COME TO THE MOUNTAIN

The seemingly fruitless existence of the monk
is therefore centered on the ultimate meaning and the highest value:
it loves the truth for its own sake, and it gives away everything
in order to hear the Word of God and do it.

—THOMAS MERTON | *Come to the Mountain, 1964*

ST. BENEDICT'S MONASTERY

COME TO THE MOUNTAIN

Fr. William Meninger, o.c.s.o.

Fr. Joseph Boyle, o.c.s.o. | Fr. Micah Schonberger, o.c.s.o.

Fr. Thomas Keating, o.c.s.o.

WITH QUOTES FROM *Come to the Mountain* © 1964 BY

Fr. Thomas Merton, o.c.s.o.

ST. BENEDICT'S MONASTERY | SNOWMASS, COLORADO

COME TO THE MOUNTAIN

Some text selections are from 1012 *Monastery Road* by Fr. William Meninger, second edition, Lantern Books, New York, 2004, and *Come to the Mountain* by Fr. Thomas Merton, St. Benedict's Monastery, Snowmass, Colorado, 1964.

Scripture texts are from the NRSV, New International Version and Grail Psalter. Quotations from the Rule of St. Benedict (RB) are from RB 1980, Liturgical Press, Collegeville, Minnesota.

* Order of Cistercians of the Strict Observance

ISBN 978-0-9964454-4-3

PRINTED IN THE UNITED STATES

✝ ST. BENEDICT'S MONASTERY
1012 MONASTERY ROAD
SNOWMASS, COLORADO 81654

DEDICATED TO ALL THOSE

WHO HAVE GONE BEFORE US WITH THE SIGN OF FAITH,

AND WHOSE DEDICATION AND PERSEVERANCE

HAVE CONTRIBUTED TO THE LIFE AND MISSION OF

ST. BENEDICT'S MONASTERY

IN ITS FIRST SIXTY YEARS (1956–2016).

FR. THEOPHANE BOYD

BR. WALTER BRANSFIELD

FR. ANDREW JACKSON

FR. DANIEL KELLIHER

BR. BERNARD O'SHEA

BR. RAPHAEL ROBIN

BR. GEORGE TAMBURELLO

CONTENTS

INTRODUCTION

Dear Friends of St. Benedict's Monastery,

IT HAS BEEN A WORK OF LOVE preparing these pages, which describe our life here at Snowmass. The year 2016 marked our sixtieth anniversary, and it is a joy to share *Come to the Mountain* with you, whose love, caring and support have made our life here in the monastic service of the Lord possible. It is our hope that in paging through this book you will feel yourself to be a part of that life. May *Come to the Mountain* also inspire you to deepen further in your own lives our mutual prayer, love and service. May it be one more bond uniting us as we journey together into the heart of God. ✤

With a grateful heart,

—Fr. Joseph Boyle, O.C.S.O.
Abbot of St. Benedict's Monastery

SAINT BENE·DICT

LET THEM PREFER NOTHING WHATEVER TO CHRIST & MAY HE BRING US ALL ALIKE TO LIFE EVERLASTING

St. Benedict of Nursia

This icon of St. Benedict (LEFT), clothed in the black and white of the Cistercian habit, was "written" by an anonymous iconographer from North Dakota.

The cave (LOWER L) represents the beginning of St. Benedict's monastic life at Subiaco.

The monastic buildings (MIDDLE R), symbol of Monte Casino (ABOVE) Benedict's first monastery near Rome, are modeled after this monastery.

Christ (UPPER L) holds out the Gospels that are the source of Benedict's Holy Rule.

S T. BENEDICT OF NURSIA is called the "Father of Western Monasticism." He was born in Italy in the sixth century and is the author of the Rule of St. Benedict (R B), which has dominated, directed and inspired monasticism in the West since the time of Charlemagne. We know of St. Benedict by way of a biography written by Pope St. Gregory the Great fifty years after Benedict's death. St. Gregory depended heavily upon the testimony of men who had known Benedict personally.

Interestingly enough, Benedict began his monastic life as a hermit. This is symbolized in the icon by the cave in the lower left corner. He was then called from seclusion by a group of monks who wanted him as their abbot. It is noteworthy that in his rule Benedict insists that monks begin their spiritual journey by living in a community, and only when they have profited as much as possible from this kind of life ("under a rule and an abbot") should some of them be permitted to go to the solitary life.

Benedict founded the monastery of Monte Casino near Rome, whence spread Benedictine monasticism throughout Europe. ❖

Stations of the Cross in the East Cloister

Daily Schedule

Life at St. Benedict's is structured around prayer. We first establish the times for prayer; then we plan the rest of the day's activities. Prayer is the anchor. We begin the day with the Night Office or the prayer of Vigils, rising before dawn to keep watch for the Lord on behalf of all humanity.

Morning 4:15 Rise for **VIGILS** (quiet community prayer of listening to scripture and other readings)

5:30 Community meditation

6:30 Personal time for reading, study, prayer, breakfast, etc.

7:30 **LAUDS** (morning prayer) and Mass

8:30 Work

Afternoon 12:25 **SEXT** (short midday prayer) and dinner (vegetarian)

1:20 **NONE** (short afternoon prayer)

1:30 Free time for **LECTIO DIVINA** or a short siesta

2:30 Work or study and **LECTIO DIVINA**

Evening 5:00 Informal supper taken in silence

6:00 Community meditation

7:00 **VESPERS** and **COMPLINE** (evening prayer)

7:30 Great Silence (until after morning Mass)

THE BENEDICTINE LEGACY

Come let us go up

to the mountain

of the Lord

To the house of

the God of Jacob,

That He may teach us

His ways

And that we may walk

in His Paths.

—ISAIAH 2:3

This icon of Christ the Teacher, located in the atrium of the church, was "written" for St. Benedict's Monastery by a monk from a monastery on Mount Athos in Greece.

HISTORY TEACHERS from local schools often ask to bring their classes to visit the monastery. Unfortunately, what some of them are looking for is a kind of living fossil to illustrate the Middle Ages. They are often surprised and sometimes disappointed to discover that we use computers instead of goose-quill pens and modern farm machinery in place of draft horses.

It must be admitted that there is in twenty-first century Benedictine life a certain justification for their expectations. This is to be found in the sixth-century Rule of St. Benedict, which still provides the inspiration and foundations for the daily lifestyle of the monastic community. It is evident that monasteries today do not, and indeed cannot, live with literal fidelity to the provisions of a sixth-century rule. Greeting guests with a ceremonial foot-washing, accepting infants into the monastic community, inflicting physical punishment on disobedient monks, and maintaining a prison for recalcitrant monks are but a few of the Rule's provisions that are not acceptable in contemporary culture.

Over the past fifteen hundred years there have been many reforms directed toward a renewed observance of the Rule. Usually they have had varying degrees of success, but probably none of them

has succeeded in returning to a literal rendering of the sixth-century Rule.

The Vatican II document on the religious life (PERFECTAE CARITATIS) calls for religious communities to do three things in their approaches to renewal. First, they must return to the sources of the whole of the Christian life; this would mean primarily the Scriptures. Second, they must return to the primitive inspiration of their institutes; this would be primarily the Rule of St. Benedict, but would also include other contemporary monastic rules that influenced it. Third, they must adapt to the changed conditions of our times. This certainly rules out any attempt at absolute observance of the Rule as written and practiced in the sixth century.

So the question must be posed, not only today but in each successive generation: What is meant when Benedictine and Cistercian monks and nuns solemnly profess to live "according to the Rule of St. Benedict"?

The Rule itself is an adaptation of a large, previously existing body of monastic literature. In the final chapter of the Rule, St. Benedict states that his rule is actually written for beginners, but, he continues, "for anyone hastening on to the perfection of the monastic life, there are the teachings of the Holy Fathers, the observance of which will lead him to the very heights of perfection." (RB 73) St. Benedict then mentions specifically the Scriptures, the writings of the desert monastic John Cassian (360–435) and the rule that St. Basil the Great (329–379) wrote in 356 for

Advent wreath ceremony before Vespers

his own monastic institute. It is also important to acknowledge how deeply influenced the Rule of St. Benedict was by another source, the Rule of the Master, written anonymously some thirty years before St. Benedict's rule.

There is an increasingly popular movement among lay people to adapt the Rule to their lifestyle outside the monastery. Adapting is what monks have been doing since the time of St. Benedict, and they will continue to do so. Monks use the Rule as an inspiration, not unlike the manner in which we use the Wisdom literature of the Old Testament. The Rule is not a series of legal prescriptions or a code of law, but rather a tried and tested practical and spiritual tradition, brought into being so that we may "See how the Lord in his love shows us the way of life." (RB PROLOGUE)

Because it is a sixth-century document, the Rule has to be constantly reinterpreted in order to be relevant to new generations, new geographies and new cultures. Thus a visit to St. Benedict's Monastery should not be seen as an opportunity to get a glimpse of the Middle Ages. This book is intended to be a reflection in pictures of how the Rule of St. Benedict is interpreted and lived in Snowmass, Colorado, today. ❖

The Cistercian monks have been devoted since the 12th century to this contemplative life in community, but the note of solitude has never been lacking in the Cistercian life.

—THOMAS MERTON

Br. Martin calls his brother monks to Mass.

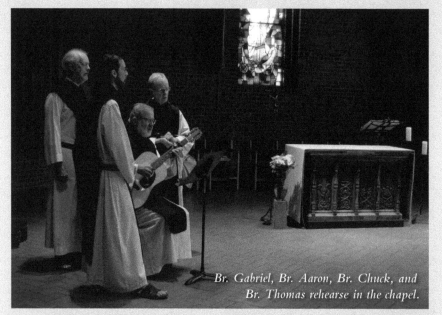

Br. Gabriel, Br. Aaron, Br. Chuck, and
Br. Thomas rehearse in the chapel.

*Brothers will read and
sing not according to
rank, but according to
their ability to benefit
their hearers.*

—RB 38

Meadowlark

Br. Chuck is an accomplished guitarist
as well as choirmaster and lead singer.

The bell tower and Mt. Sopris are symbolic of St. Benedict's.

THE PSALMS

THE BOOK OF PSALMS, also known as the Psalter, is the prayer book of the Church. It is also the prayer book of the monk. In the Rule of St. Benedict (R B), it is expected that the entire Psalter will be committed to memory. The psalms, all one hundred and fifty of which St. Benedict expected to be chanted each week, do present several problems. They were composed over a period of 1,500 years and express the theology, culture, aspirations, expectations and even the weaknesses of the Old Testament era. A literal interpretation of some of them is even quite incompatible with Christian teachings.

Nonetheless, the psalms are a part of the inspired word of God and therefore must be seen as compatible with the life and teachings of the Word Made Flesh, Jesus Christ. By the time of the R B, it was a well-developed practice to see the psalms on four different levels. First, there is the literal interpretation: What do the words mean as the author intended them? Second, there is the Christological interpretation: How the psalms predict the coming of Christ and how they can be seen as embodying his teachings. Third, there is the moral sense: How are the psalms to be applied to the daily life of the monk? Fourth, there is the eschatological level, in which the psalms are seen as somehow referring to the full accomplishment of the Kingdom of God.

St. John Cassian, Marseille, France 360-435 AD

St. Benedict was very familiar with the writings of an earlier monk, John Cassian, who explained the four senses by using as an example the city of Jerusalem. In the first or literal sense, Jerusalem refers to the capital city of the Jews. In the second or Christological sense, it refers to the Church of Christ. In the third or moral sense, Jerusalem is seen as the soul struggling to embody and provide a dwelling place for God. In the fourth or eschatological sense, the city is seen as the heavenly Jerusalem descending from above as a bride adorned in wedding garments without spot or wrinkle. Sometimes the levels are made simpler by referring to the first as the literal interpretation and the second, third and fourth as the allegorical interpretations.

For the monk, the psalms cover the entire gamut of experiences the monastic life is intended to elicit. This includes a simple appreciation of the beauties of nature, an awesome response to the power of God in violent storms, earthquakes and even wars. The psalms express for the monk his experiences of contemplative wonder and his fear of the majesty of God as well as his tender response to the paternal love of his creator and redeemer. They allow him to speak of his disappointments, illnesses, failures and sins, of his fear of the unknown and of the persecutions he suffers in his attempts to serve the Lord. No human emotion is missing from them, and they call forth every possible grace-filled aspiration. ❖

Thus one could see in these places as it were an altogether different country, cut off from the rest of the world, and the fortunate inhabitants of that country had no other thought than to live in love and justice.

—St. Athanasius,
Life of St. Anthony
of the Desert

This Madonna has watched over the corral for over 60 years.

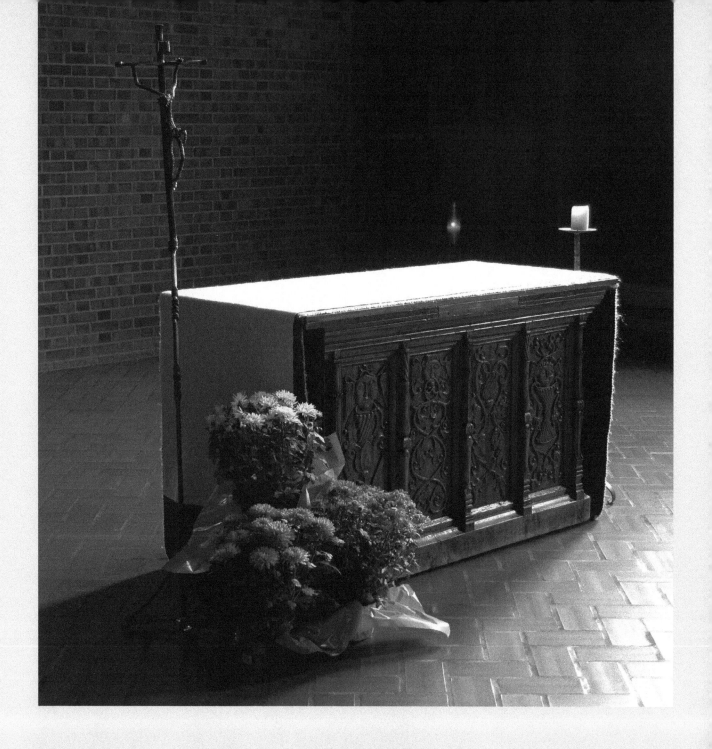

COMPLINE

The oratory ought to be what it is called and nothing else is to be said or done there. After the Work of God all should leave in complete silence and with reverence for God, so that a brother who may wish to pray alone will not be disturbed.

—RB 52

The high altar dates from fourteenth-century England.

THE MONASTIC DAY ENDS with the office of Compline. Here at St. Benedict's Monastery Compline follows Vespers after a brief period of silent prayer. The monks will assemble again at 4:30 a.m. for the night office (Vigils). The long interval between Compline and Lauds in the morning is one of complete silence—even to the avoidance of eye contact.

Br. Raymond

At the conclusion of Compline, the Salve Regina is sung and the abbot prays, "May the Lord grant you a quiet night and a peaceful death." The monks reply, "Amen." This is followed by a blessing of each monk with holy water as a reminder of his baptismal cleansing. ✤

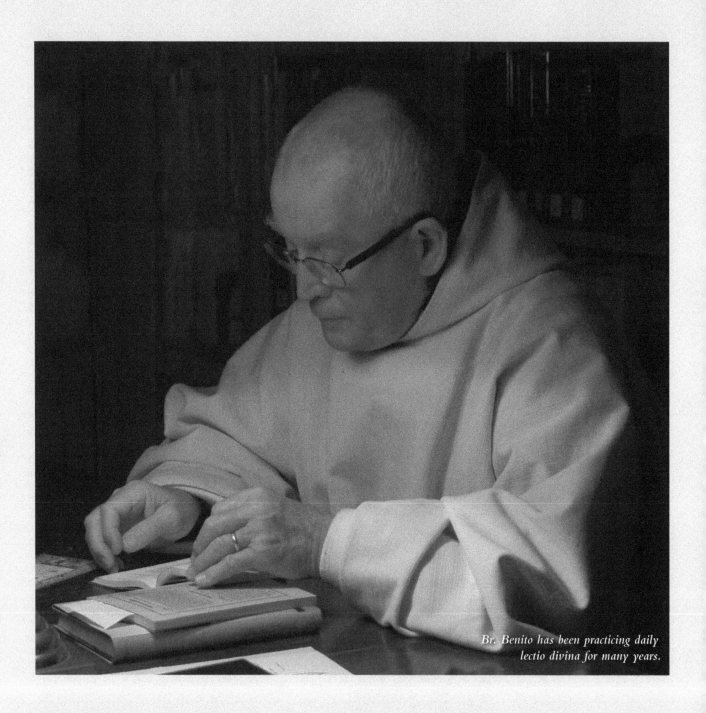

Br. Benito has been practicing daily lectio divina for many years.

LECTIO DIVINA

FOR MONKS, lectio divina, sometimes inaccurately translated as spiritual reading, is an all-embracing term. It covers the entire gamut of the monastic understanding of our relationship with God. It embraces the remotest sources for prayer, starting with our experience of the providence of God in our daily lives. Anything approached with faith can be a source of lectio divina. This can include our experiences of nature, as both beautiful and awesomely terrifying; the study of science; the reading of history, novels or poetry; the blessings and tragedies of our personal relationships; and all of the other ways, both subtle and blunt, in which God touches our lives.

Lectio involves all of our faculties, physical and spiritual. It is especially directed toward focusing our intellect, memory and imagination as well as our passions and instinctual powers on the presence, activity and loving providence of God as he reveals himself to us. In a special way, lectio is presented to the monk in the scriptures, the liturgy and the writings of the monastic fathers and mothers, both old and new. Frequently these three sources are combined in the monastic liturgy, the divine office that outlines the monk's day, beginning with the night office (performed before dawn) and ending with evening prayer (Compline).

St. Benedict delivering his Rule in 1129 to St. Maurus and other monks of his order, from a manuscript at the Monastery of St. Gilles, Nimes, France.

The intervals in a monk's day, those periods of time when he is not engaged in either liturgical prayer or in work, are considered lectio time (rather than "free" time). By its very nature, lectio leads to meditation, in which the monk reflects on the meaning of its content for his personal life and the world he lives in. This calls for what monks term "holy leisure," i.e. time to be alone and quiet in order to enter into an awareness and a meaningful acceptance of God's action in our lives. The entire monastic structure, or what is called in sociological terms the controlled environment of the monastery, is oriented toward providing and protecting this space. The monk must be constantly aware of the danger of allowing the "busyness" of daily labor from encroaching on this sacred task.

The next step after meditatio is oratio, or prayer, properly so called. This occurs when the monk's lectio, by way of meditation, permeates his understanding, emotions and even his instinctual levels of knowing. He is then led to express this concretely in a personal relationship with God. This is expressed in the words that form his oratio, or prayer. This prayer can be a carefully reasoned, faith-inspired colloquy with God or it can be by way of formal liturgical or devotional prayers ("read" prayers such as the rosary, novena, etc.) or even at times by an effusive, emotion-laden outpouring of faith, hope and love.

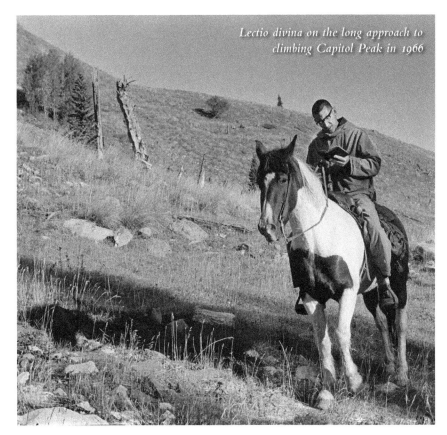
Lectio divina on the long approach to climbing Capitol Peak in 1966

Prayer is a dialogue.
It involves a give and take,
a listening and a speaking.
God speaks to us,
we listen;
we speak,
God listens to us.
It really is as simple
as that.

—WILLIAM MENINGER

The next step in the lectio process is contemplatio, or contemplation. This comes about when the physical, intellectual and emotional faculties cease to be adequate and the will (the loving faculty) seeks and is given in faith a union with God—a union that comes about in a darkness that is not the absence of light but the presence of too much light. The monk then experiences the truth of the spiritual maxim "he whom the mind cannot grasp the heart can embrace." This is referred to as the contemplative experience. In the monastic tradition these four steps (lectio, meditatio, oratio, contemplatio) are really one process, simply called lectio divina.

Suggested steps for an effective use of the Scriptures in lectio divina:

Work as prayer...Fr. Micah builds a bookcase.

❶ BUILD A CHURCH | Create for yourself a special environment in which you will recognize that you are doing something different and special, something that will bring you into God's presence. This can be done by going into your bedroom, closing the door, and lighting a candle. It can be done simply by kneeling down in a private place, offering a brief prayer to be attentive to God's word, and then kissing the Bible and sitting down to listen.

❷ BE AWARE THAT GOD has already spoken. You could not even begin this prayerful reading if God had not first summoned you to it by his grace. "No one can say Jesus is Lord unless he be given the power by the Holy Spirit" (SEE 1 CORINTHIANS 12:3). You are already into your prayer. God has called you and you have answered by going apart, taking your Bible, and starting your prayer. Now it is God's turn again.

❸ ALLOW GOD NOW TO SPEAK through the Scriptures. Open the Bible to the psalms or the Gospels. Read, listen to what God says for a verse or two until you wish to stop and respond. He is speaking to you.

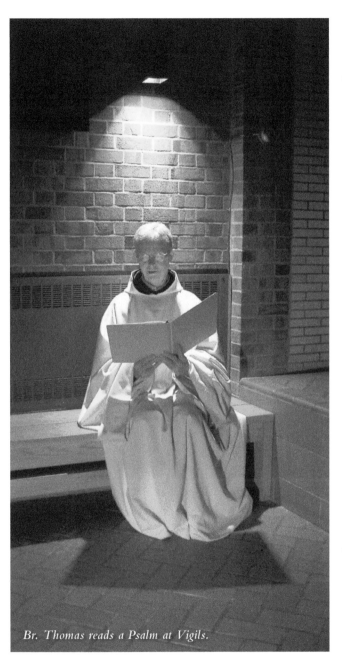

Br. Thomas reads a Psalm at Vigils.

④ PRAYER IS A DIALOGUE | Speak to God. Ask him for an understanding of the text. Ask him how it applies to you. Listen again to what he says in your heart, the Scriptural texts, or both, and then respond again as you would in any conversation.

⑤ DECIDE BEFOREHAND how long you want to pray. Maybe ten or fifteen minutes are enough. When your time is up, thank God for his presence and his wisdom. Be prepared, when you can, to extend the conversation if you feel so inclined.

Prayer is a dialogue. It involves a give and take, a listening and a speaking. God speaks to us, we listen; we speak, God listens to us. It really is as simple as that. We must, however, realize that what God says to us is of extreme importance. We must give him the opportunity to speak and we must give ourselves the opportunity to listen.

Jesus is the Word. He is the Father's response (dialogue) to all of our needs. Through him the Father is always speaking in human accents the very fullness of what he is. He is saying everything from the fiat of creation

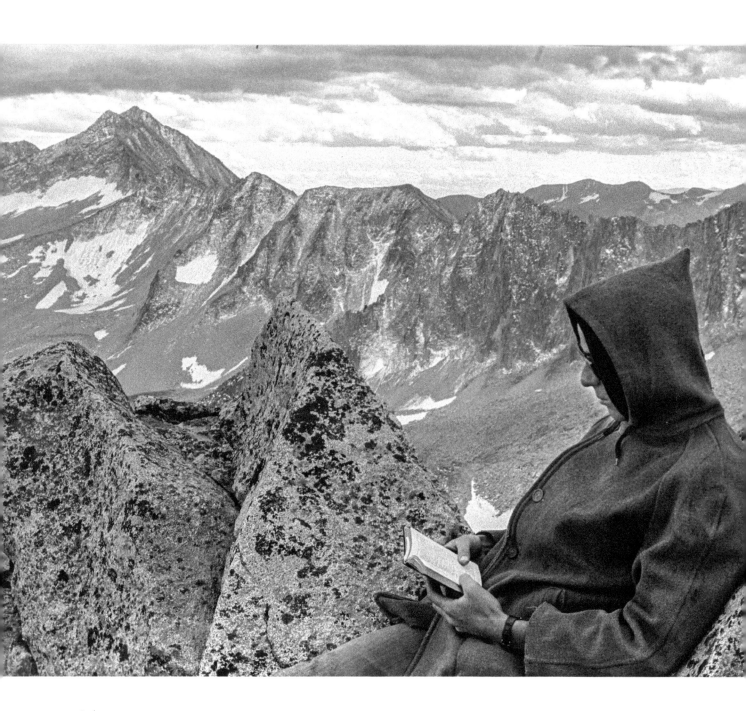

to the bestowing of grace in all of its forms on humanity to the very final Amen, which announces the complete fullness of his kingdom. To adapt the opening of the Gospel of St. John:

The Word dwelt with God, and what God was, the Word was. The Word then was with God at the beginning, and through him all things came to be. No single thing was created without him. All that came to be was alive with his life, and that life was the light of men.

Because God is Father, he is personal. His word is addressed to every single individual in a personal way, responding to every need in every situation. Do we need to praise God? Do we need comfort? Do we need to be rebuked, loved, reassured, chastised, instructed, pacified? God always speaks the word that we need to hear (and not always what we want to hear).

Using the Scriptures is an important and helpful way to listen to God and hear, beyond the chatter of daily life, what he is saying to us. ❖

It is a total consciousness and awareness of God which is impossible without silence, recollection, solitude, and a certain withdrawal.

—THOMAS MERTON

With Snowmass Mountain (14,098′) in the distance, Fr. Joseph practices lectio divina near Capitol Peak, 1966.

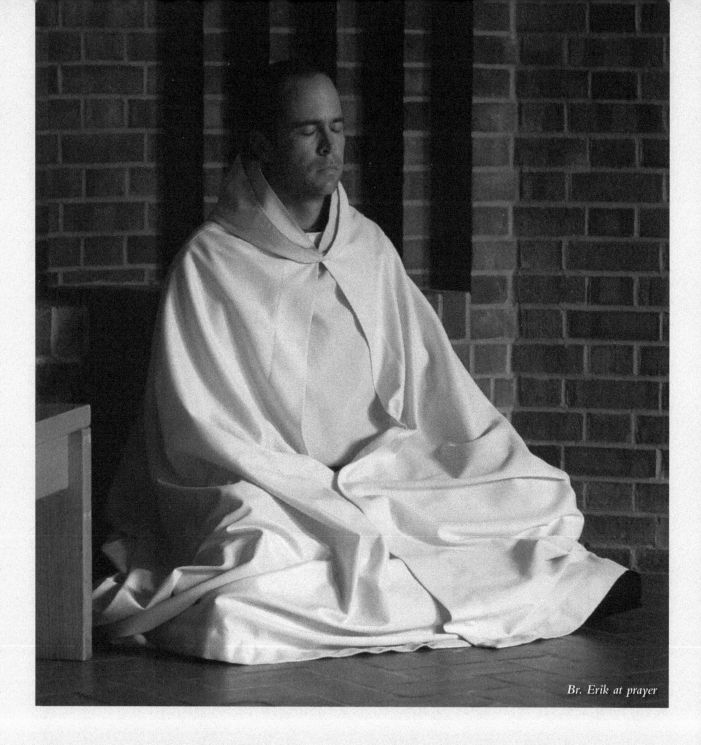

Br. Erik at prayer

CONTEMPLATION

...for contemplation is received in obedience to the Holy Spirit and one cannot obey Him unless he has first learned to recognize His will manifested through human superiors.

—THOMAS MERTON

OFFICIALLY, at least, the monks of our community are contemplatives. We are said to belong to a contemplative order. But what does that mean? Part of the answer may be seen any morning in our darkened church from 4 to 5 a.m. The still figures of the white-clad monks can barely be made out scattered here and there throughout the church. Some are sitting on cushions on the floor, others more traditionally are seated in the choir. Until the clock in the cloister chimes the half-hour, there is not a stir. Then the monks arise and begin a silent, ten-minute walking meditation, covering the full circuit of the church, until they once again reach their original seats. Again they take their preferred positions and resume their meditations.

But is this contemplation? Are the monks engaged in contemplative prayer? There is no way to answer that question on an individual basis except by asking each individual monk. Certainly they are taught the principles of contemplative prayer and there is a certain presumption even before they enter the monastery that deep prayer is a part of their lives.

Perhaps there are better words to describe the monks or the monastic lifestyle. Some prefer "a contemplative attitude" to "contemplation." This extends contemplation from something done merely at assigned prayer times to an attitude of listening to God that extends throughout the day. Still others feel that "a monastic lifestyle" is sufficient. At any rate, contemplative prayer is sometimes easier to experience than to describe.

In chapters eighteen and nineteen of the First Book of Kings we read the fascinating account of the prophet Elijah and Queen Jezebel. Jezebel was the wife of Ahab, who had married her in spite of the prohibition forbidding Israelites to marry Philistines. To make matters worse, when Jezebel came to assume the throne of Israel she brought with her four hundred and fifty prophets of Baal and four hundred priests of the goddess Asherah.

Elijah was fed up with King Ahab's fence sitting. "If Yahweh is God, serve him," he declared. "If Baal is, then follow him." Then Elijah told Ahab to summon all of Israel together with all of Jezebel's pagan priests and prophets to meet with him on Mt. Carmel. It was time for a showdown.

Elijah had two altars built and told the people to bring two bulls for sacrifice. The pagans were to prepare one bull and lay it on the wood without setting fire to it. Then they were to invoke Baal to cause a fire to consume their offering. Elijah would do likewise and call upon Yahweh. The one who answered by fire was to be recognized as God.

So from morning until noon the priests called upon Baal by name, "Baal, Baal, answer us." But there was no reply. They shouted louder and, as was their custom, danced with abandon around the altar. All afternoon they ranted and raved and gashed themselves with knives and spears until the hour of the evening sacrifice. Still there was no reply, no sound, no sign of awareness.

Elijah then prepared his bull, laid it upon the wood, and told the Israelites to fill four jars with water and pour them over the animal and the wood. They did this three times, and the water ran over the altar and filled the trench Elijah had ordered to be dug around it. Then Elijah stepped forward and offered a simple prayer to Yahweh. Suddenly the fire of the Lord fell from out of the heavens and consumed the whole offering and the wood. It licked up the water in the trench and scorched the very stones of the altar and the earth on which it stood. When the people saw this they fell on their faces and cried, "Yahweh is God, Yahweh is God."

Those to whom Christ gives spiritual nourishment (in the grace of prayer) He first makes truly obedient.

—St. Aelred

Elijah is the patron of mountain chapels.

Here he is fed by a crow while he awaits a theophany, a vision of God, outside his mountain cave.

This icon was "written" for the monastery by a friend from South Dakota.

At this point, Elijah ordered the people to seize the prophets of Baal, take them down to the wadi at Kishon and slaughter them there in the valley.

Ahab rushed to his wife Jezebel and told her all that Elijah had done and how he had put all of her prophets to the sword. Enraged, Jezebel sent a messenger to Elijah. "May the gods curse me," she said, "if by this time tomorrow I have not taken your life as you took theirs." Elijah was afraid and fled for his life.

But his troubles had just begun. He got as far as Beersheba in Judea where he despaired and asked the Lord to take his life. Instead, the Lord sent an angel to give him bread and water. He ate and drank and, nourished by this food, went on for forty days and forty nights until he reached Horeb, the mountain of God. (Horeb is another name for Mt. Sinai.) Elijah entered a cave and waited. He was told to go and stand on the mountain before God, who would pass by.

Suddenly a great and strong wind came, rending the earth and shattering the very rocks before him. But the Lord was not in the wind. And after the wind there was an earthquake, which made the mountain tremble and caused the stones to fall in an awesome landslide, but the Lord was not in the earthquake. And after the earthquake, fire, but the Lord was not in the fire. Then Elijah heard the sound of a gentle breeze, and when he heard it he hid his face in his cloak and went out and stood at the mouth of his cave. Then a voice spoke to him, and this was the voice of God.

If we wish to enter heaven with Jesus and through Him, we must leave this world in thought & contemplation; we must also, if we can, raise our hearts above the senses of the flesh, and take up the bright armor of obedience.

—ST. AELRED OF RIEVAULX

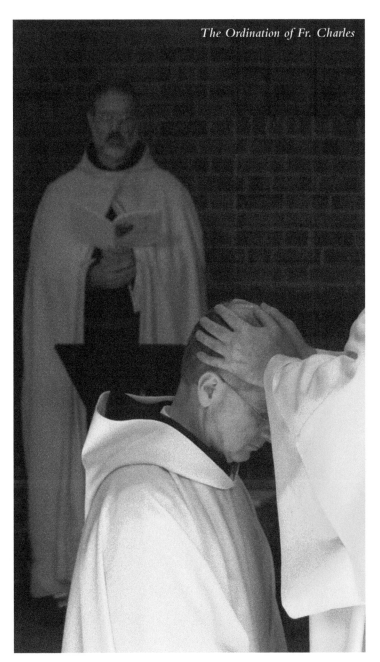

The Ordination of Fr. Charles

Something very interesting is happening here. There is a deliberate contrast shown in the manner in which God spoke to Elijah and in the manner in which he had spoken to Moses and the people in the past. The author of the First Book of Kings wants us to see Elijah in terms of the past, but with a difference.

During the time of their sojourn in the desert, the Israelites had been a crass, ignorant people who could only be brought to God by fear and a display of his power. When the Lord promised to speak to them (EXODUS 19), Moses was told to put barriers around the mountain. Any person or animal who so much as touched the edge of the mountain was to be stoned. And there were peals of thunder and flashes of lightning, dense clouds, and a loud blast of trumpets. The people waiting at the foot of the mountain were terrified. The sound of the trumpets grew ever louder, and whenever Moses spoke, the Lord answered him in peals of thunder.

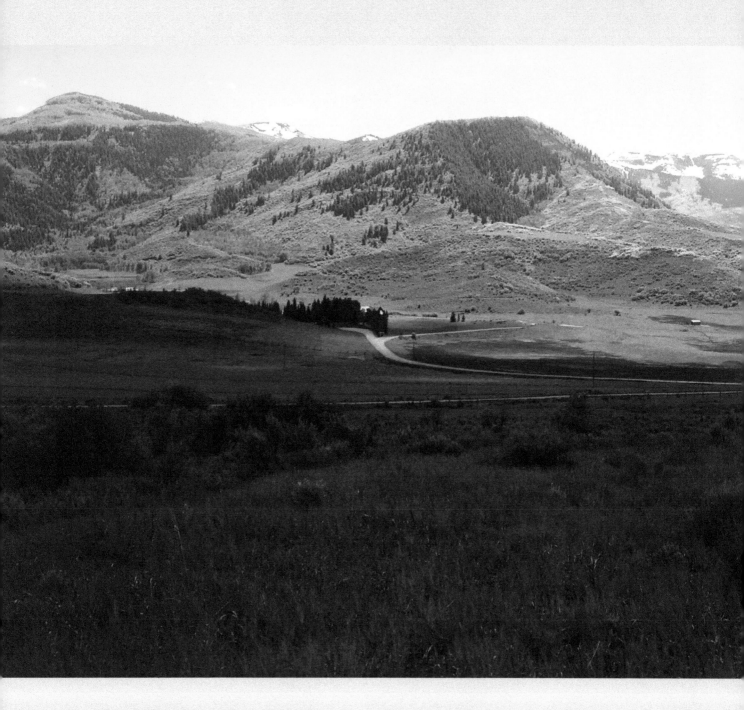

Note the similarities between the story of Moses and the story of Elijah. Moses and the people were fleeing persecution from a pagan ruler; Elijah was fleeing persecution from Jezebel. Moses wandered in the desert for forty years; Elijah wandered in the desert for forty days and forty nights. Moses and the people were fed by a miracle from God; Elijah was given food and drink by an angel. Both were told to go to Mt. Sinai where God would meet and speak to them.

Here, however, the similarities end. The contrast now is quite deliberate and is repeated in three different ways. God will no longer speak to his people through fear. He is explicitly said not to have been in the wind, the earthquake, or the fire. Rather now he is recognized in quiet, in the peaceful sound of a gentle breeze.

We can take this story one step further, to another mountain at another time. On Mt. Tabor we have the same cast. Elijah and Moses are talking to Jesus. And suddenly there is a cloud and from the cloud the voice of God speaks. His command is a step further even than hearing him in the silence of Elijah. His command now is to accept Jesus as his beloved son and listen to him.

This is contemplative prayer, listening to God. Not only listening to God but also hearing him, and especially hearing him in silence, beyond words and without images. ✤

Go out into the hill country and bring back branches from olive and wild olive trees, and from myrtles, palms and shade trees.

—NEHEMIAH 8

No "olive, myrtles, or palms," but plenty of "shade trees" at 7,760' in Snowmass, Colorado.

Rule of St. Benedict
France • 12th century manuscript

The Rule of St. Benedict

As for God,

his way is perfect.

The word of the

Lord is flawless.

He is a shield for all

who take refuge in him.

—Psalm 18

THE MONKS OF SNOWMASS, as do all Cistercian monks, follow the Rule of St. Benedict (RB). This rule tells a fascinating story in its passage through time, tradition and history from Benedict's monastery at Monte Casino to St. Benedict's monastery at Snowmass, Colorado. Benedict intended his rule to reflect the monastic tradition received from the desert monks of Egypt, St. Jerome and the monasticism of Palestine, John Cassian in Gaul, and especially St. Basil in Cappadocia.

Borrowing from many sources, especially from an ancient document known as the Rule of the Master, the RB has been accepted as the normative guide for almost all western monasteries. By the eleventh century it had become the basis for the reformed monasticism lived in the great abbey of Cluny in France and in its hundreds of affiliated communities throughout Europe.

In 1098, St. Robert of the Cluniac monastery of Molesme in France and a handful of other monks, feeling that the Cluniac reform had deviated from the spirit of the Rule of St. Benedict because of an excessive stress on the liturgical celebration of the divine office, founded a new monastery near Dijon in France,

It is the peculiar office of the monk in the modern world to keep alive the Contemplative experience and to keep the way open for modern technological people to recover the integrity of their own inner depths.

—THOMAS MERTON

known as Citeaux. This was not a reform necessitated by a laxity in the observance practiced by the Cluniacs. Rather it was an attempt to go back to the simplicity of the contemplative attitude of the Rule. Thus, there was now an emphasis on simplicity, silence, solitude and contemplation by way of lectio divina. This reform, which constituted the founding of the Cistercian order, spread widely in the Western Church until it itself fell into decline. Ravaged by the Reformation and internal negligence, the Order underwent a further reform in the seventeenth century at the monastery of La Trappe near Paris. This new Trappist reform, with its emphasis on acts of penitence rather than contemplation, quickly spread throughout Europe, establishing new houses and greatly influencing most religious orders. Since the Second Vatican Council (1962–1965) there has been yet another movement within the Trappists to return to the contemplative ideals of the early Cistercians.

Fr. Thomas Merton wrote the original Come to the Mountain *in 1964.*

St. Joseph's Abbey in Spencer, Massachusetts was one of the many monasteries of the Trappist reform that flourished after World War II and beyond because of the influence of the writings of Thomas

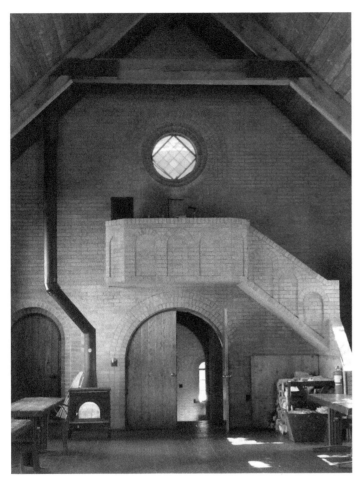

The refectory and reader's pulpit

Merton (1915–1968). From Spencer the Rule of St. Benedict was brought to Snowmass, Colorado by way of the foundation of St. Benedict's Monastery in 1956.

The Rule is known and appreciated for its compassion and moderation, especially in view of the severity of its predecessors in the Middle East, France and Ireland. A classic example of this moderation is found in chapter forty where Benedict legislates on the proper amount of food and drink for monks. He first apologizes and admits to a certain uneasiness in specifying the amount of food and drink for others. Then, he writes, with "due regard for the infirmities of the sick" a half bottle of wine a day is enough for each. He goes on to say that monks should not drink wine at all, but "since the monks of the day cannot be convinced of this," they should at least agree to drink in moderation. The R B is intended to be a practical, concrete way to live out the teachings of the Gospels in an intense communal situation. ❖

MONKS AND LABOR

…manual labor in the fields has something of a solitary and prayerful character, besides which it enables the monk to be to some extent self-sustaining and thus to be free of multiple contacts with the outside world.

—THOMAS MERTON

IN HIS RULE, St. Benedict affirms the importance of physical labor in the life of the monk. "When they live by the labor of their hands, as our fathers and the apostles did, they are truly monks." (RB 48) Periods of the day set aside for labor are given a balanced emphasis, with time set aside for prayer. "Idleness is the enemy of the soul. Therefore the brothers should have specified periods for manual labor as well as for prayerful reading." (RB 48)

Monks' efforts to live by the labor of their hands have taken many different forms in the history of monastic houses. The most obvious and, in some ways, the most ideal form of labor is agrarian. Today, however, farming in monasteries has become almost a luxury. At one time at St. Benedict's Monastery the entire community could be seen in the fields in the evening, harvesting oats or hay, rounding up cattle or herding sheep. Today with modern farming techniques, most of this work can be done by two or three monks.

Monks have now turned to small industries (sometimes,

Cattle roundup • Fall 1966

Br. Aaron in the bookstore

Fr. Ed adjusts a sprinkler head

…the importance of daily manual labour appropriate to the ability of the monk. The hours of labour vary with the season but are never less than five hours a day.

—RB 48

Br. Benito chops under the watchful eye of St. Pasquale.

Br. Erik, Fr. Charlie, and Br. Evan baking cookies

Br. Erik mops the cloister hall

*Like archers, they aim past all these targets.
They are in the business of serving God
by serving one another and their neighbors.
They are spiritual people who happen to run
businesses; they are not profit-driven people who
happen to have a sideline interest in service
for public relations purposes.*

—AUGUST TURAK | Buisness Secrets of the Trappists • *Forbes*

By the time Br. Raymond bought the road grader in 1995, it was already thirty years old.

not so small) such as baking, bookbinding, bee keeping, carpentry, even making coffins. Efforts at earning our living here at St. Benedict's have take the forms of cow-calf operations, production of hard candies and a small eggery. Unable to compete with larger commercial equivalents, we now focus on boarding cattle, farming a special quality hay for local horses, running a small cookie bakery and a book store, and maintaining a moderately sized but very active retreat facility. The monks are encouraged also to develop and express their individual interests and talents by writing, working in the carpentry shop, designing greeting cards, taking photographs, and so on.

Land is important for Cistercian monastic living. St. Benedict's has over three thousand acres of ranch land, farm buildings, hay fields, forests and pasturage. This puts the monks in touch with present-day ecological concerns and responsibilities to the larger surrounding community. It also provides us with the opportunity to share our spacious and beautiful valley with the hundreds of guests who visit us yearly. ❖

From May to September, Br. Evan and other brothers move the side-roll sprinklers daily.

…the joy of the monastic life comes from generous sharing in a common spiritual task of praise and labor, and a common search for truth.

—THOMAS MERTON

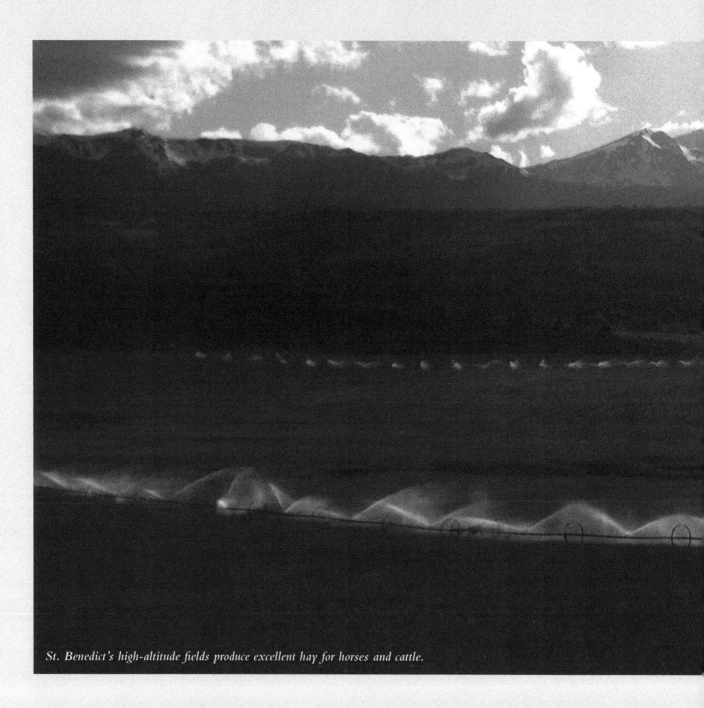

St. Benedict's high-altitude fields produce excellent hay for horses and cattle.

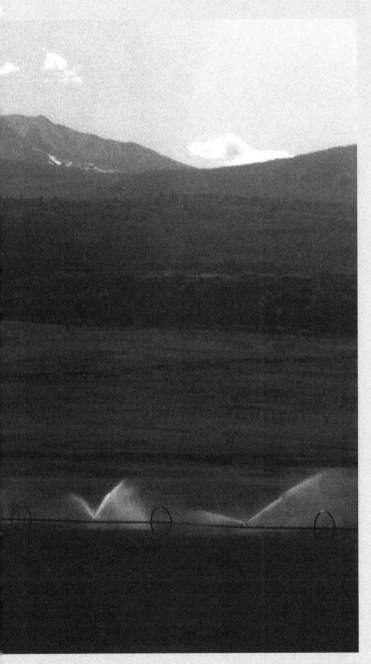

*The fact remains that there are men
truly called as Abraham was to
leave their homes, to depart from
the cities of men, to renounce even
the active Christian life in those
cities, and to become henceforth
strangers in the world, living apart,
consecrated to silent meditation
and liturgical praise,
to poverty, manual labor, solitude,
sacred study and spiritual discipline.*

—Thomas Merton

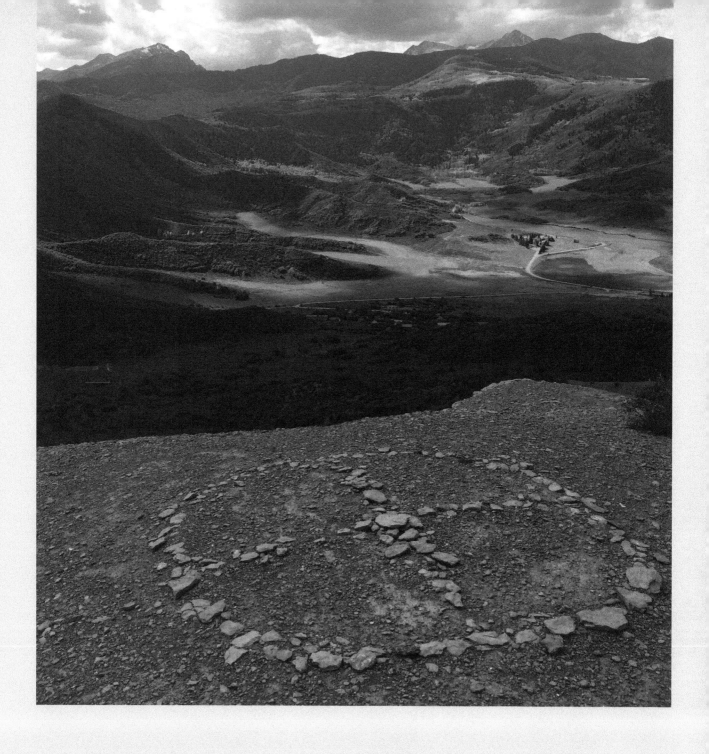

*The heavens proclaim
your glory, O God,
and the firmament
shows forth the work
of your hands.*

—PSALM 19

EVA is our monastery cat, though we are not quite sure if she belongs to us or if we belong to her. I say we are not sure because there is no doubt at all in her mind. We, the monastery, the ranch, and the entire valley exist only for her benefit. We definitely get the feeling that Eva uses us. In her cat-mind we exist for the sole purpose of filling her dish. We are also allowed to open the kitchen door a hundred times a day for her comings and goings. Possessing nothing, she lives as owner of all she surveys, and she may well be the most integrated inhabitant of the monastery.

But then it seems that all the animals in this Eden Garden of the Rocky Mountains have the same attitude. Is this perhaps a reversal of roles stemming from original sin? Are the animals, once created to serve man, now his masters? It certainly seemed so to Br. Benito when he arose before midnight in the sub-zero February night to see if the

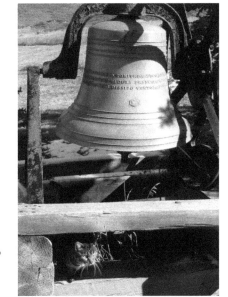

*Viewed from Bernie's Rock (8,648')
the monastery captures a patch of
sunlight.*

Elk cross St. Benedict's hay fields

ewes needed his help in dropping their lambs. The novices feel the same way, no doubt, when they, each in his turn, have to hurry down to the barnyard before our 4:30 AM night office to bring a bottle of warm milk to our first-born lamb, Agatha, who lost her mother at birth. Indeed, the normal course of our winter work day here at St. Benedict's Monastery is spent mostly in the service of "our" animals: cows, horses, sheep, pigs, and chickens.

The wild animals are no more subservient. Obviously the herd of elk, two hundred strong, that appears almost miraculously in our oat field every October evening feels that the property is theirs. Of course, they were here long before we were, but must they be so disdainful, hopping over our five-foot-high fences as though they did not exist? And the mule deer are not to be trusted either. By sheer numbers alone they lay claim to our land. After all, what can eighteen squatter monks say to eight hundred deer about living space?

And then there are the coyotes. Not only do they claim prior rights to our sheep, but they loudly howl their ownership into the night air from the fields adjacent to our monastic cells. The snowshoe rabbits and the prairie dogs own our roads. The rabbits race our farm vehicles between the road and the irrigation ditches, while the prairie dogs dig their dens right in the middle of the roads.

And the porcupines! Who ever told them that we were raising an acre of broccoli just for their supper? I'm sure Br. Kevin hoped to dissuade them of this notion when he trapped eight of them in the garden last August. We won't even mention the owls who steal our piglets, nor the field mice who invade our greenhouse and try to homestead in this bonanza of succulent crops.

What does all this say to us? We have but to look at Psalm 104, which we sing in choir each week:

Thou dost make the springs break out in the gullies,
    so that their water runs between the hills.
The wild beasts all drink from them,
    the wild asses quench their thirst;
The birds of the air nest on their banks
    and sing among the leaves.
From the high pavilion thou dost water the hills;
    The earth is enriched by thy provision.
Thou makest grass to grow for the cattle,
    and green things for those who toil for man,
bringing bread out of the earth
    and wine to gladden men's hearts,
oil to make their faces shine
    and bread to sustain their strength. . . .
When thou makest darkness and it is night,

O God our savior, the hope of all the ends of the earth and of the distant seas, you set the mountains in place by your power.

—PSALM 65

Thou makest grass to grow for the cattle...

all the beasts of the forest come forth;

the young lions roar for their prey,

seeking their food from God.

When thou makest the sun rise,

they slink away and go to rest in their lairs;

but man comes out to his work,

and to his labors until evening.

Countless are the things thou hast made, O Lord.

Perhaps, after all, we are not the masters that we think we are. Or maybe we have simply misunderstood what mastery is. Is it the mastery of domination, by which we stand above all creation and demand that it serve us at whatever cost? Or is it the kind of mastery that God has shown us in the Incarnation, whereby we become part of creation and contribute to a mutually beneficial service?

What a different kind of world this delineates for us; a holistic, ecological balance in which men and women take their rightful share—one of mastery because it is one of intelligent stewardship—in which they work together with all creation.

Countless are the things thou hast made, O Lord.

Thou hast made all by thy wisdom; and the earth is full of thy creatures, beasts great and small.

Adam was created from the earth. He is a part of it. Raised to mastery over all creatures because he is in the image and likeness of God, he uses that dominion and reflects that likeness by exercising the very wisdom of God who tells him, "Be wise, my son, then you will bring joy to my heart." (PROVERBS 27:11)

How much we can learn from our fellow creatures! How perfectly they serve the Creator simply by being manifestations of his wisdom!

Let the fields be jubilant, and everything in them. Then all the trees of the forest will sing for joy.

—PSALM 96

Four things there are which are smallest on earth yet wise beyond the wisest: ants, a people with no strength, yet they prepare their store of food in the summer; rock-badgers, a feeble folk, yet they make their home among the rocks; locusts, which have no king, yet they all sally forth in detachments; the lizard, which can be grasped in the hand, yet is found in the palaces of kings." (PROVERBS 30:24–28)

Cottontail rabbit

The ants, the rock-badgers, the locusts, and the lizard—all insignificant in the hierarchy of creation—serve God perfectly by their response to his wisdom. Men and women alone are free to sin, to be unloving, to abuse their mastery. We are a part of creation, but by reason of our intelligence we are its cutting edge. We are in the forefront and have much to say in determining its direction.

A few years ago we were privileged to receive a visit from Dr. Mortimer Adler (1902–2001), who used to summer in nearby Aspen. He spoke to us about the function and capacity of the human mind. There are, he told us, four levels of activity in the human mind. The first is information. The mind in this regard is like an encyclopedia or a computer; it gathers and stores information, a series of facts. The second level is knowledge. The mind takes the information or series of facts and categorizes them, puts them in order, and gives them organization, value and importance. (And now we are beyond the computer's capabilities.) The third level is understanding. The Scriptures tell us that "knowledge is the principal thing; therefore, get knowledge; but in all thy getting, get understanding." On this level we are enabled to live our knowledge, to have experience of it and to use it in our daily lives. Finally, the fourth and highest mental activity is wisdom. This enables us to see our information, knowledge and understanding in the light of ultimate goals, in the view of eternity, from the very perspective of God. As God made all things in wisdom, so we must see creation and our part in it from the viewpoint of God's purpose. It is surely in this sense that we may understand Jesus' statement: "The kingdom of God is within you."

This is the kind of wisdom that goes beyond textbooks and universities. It was a basic part of the life of Native Americans, who would not kill a deer for food without praying to its spirit to explain their need and their gratitude, and who would permit nothing of their quarry to be wasted. This is the wisdom that comes from the simplicity of babes and infants. Unless we become like them, we shall not enter the Kingdom of God. It is the fruit not so much of study as of prayer:

"My son, if you take my words to heart and lay up my commands in your mind, giving your attention to wisdom and your mind to understanding, if you summon discernment

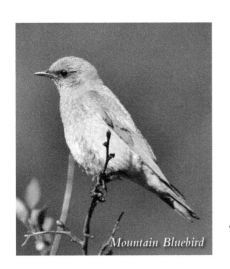

Mountain Bluebird

Sing to God,
sing praise to his name,
extol him who rides
on the clouds.
His name is the Lord
and rejoice before him

—PSALM 68

to your aid and invoke understanding, if you seek her out like silver and dig for her like buried treasure, then you will understand the fear of the Lord and attain to the knowledge of God; for the Lord bestows wisdom and teaches knowledge and understanding." (PROVERBS 2:1–6)

"In wisdom the Lord founded the earth." (PROVERBS 3:13) and it is through the wise that he brings it to its appointed fullness. This fullness will manifest itself in the establishment of his kingdom, not only in the hearts of a few simple and wise people but eventually everywhere and in everyone.

As far as the heavens are from the earth, so far are God's ways from our ways. The kingdom will not be dependent on the great and powerful of this world but on the wise, the humble and the simple. We see it now only in part and in a dark mirror, but we do see it, and we can enter into it, share it and advance it. Each one of us has his or her place in bringing about the fullness of God's kingdom. ❖

Mt. Sopris (12,953') is just a few miles from the monastery fields.

GUESTS

All guests who present themselves are to be welcomed as Christ, for he himself will say, "I was a stranger and you welcomed me (Mt 25:35)."

—RB 53

GUESTS, according to the Rule of St. Benedict (RB), are to be welcomed as Christ, especially pilgrims and the poor. The rich, by reason of the very awe they inspire, will guarantee themselves special respect. The abbot and the entire community are told to wash the feet of the guests. Here we can clearly see how the RB needs to be reinterpreted according to the signs of the times.

It is as true today as it was in Benedict's day that monasteries are "never without guests." The RB comes from a time before motels and "bed and breakfast" houses proliferated. Commercial travelers and pilgrims especially presented monks with the opportunity to feed the hungry and shelter the homeless.

As important as they were, guests were nonetheless to be kept separate from the monastic community in order to protect the environment of prayer. Most often today guests come under the category of retreatants, i.e. not people who are in temporary need of shelter on their journey but people

Ding Room at the Retreat Center

Mt. Sopris rises above the Prayer Hall at the Retreat Center.

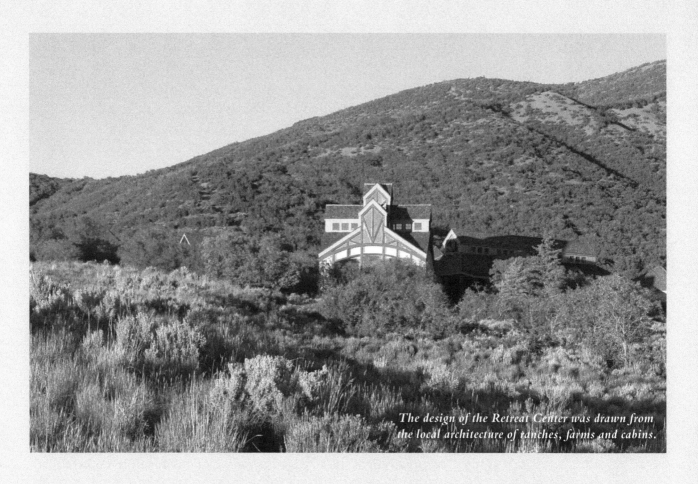

The design of the Retreat Center was drawn from the local architecture of ranches, farms and cabins.

As a place where people could come and share the peaceful setting of the Capitol Creek Valley, we sometimes called the Retreat Center the "half-way house" between the noisy, busy outside world and the silence and contemplation found at the Monastery.

— MICHAEL FULLER | Architect • St. Benedict's Retreat Center

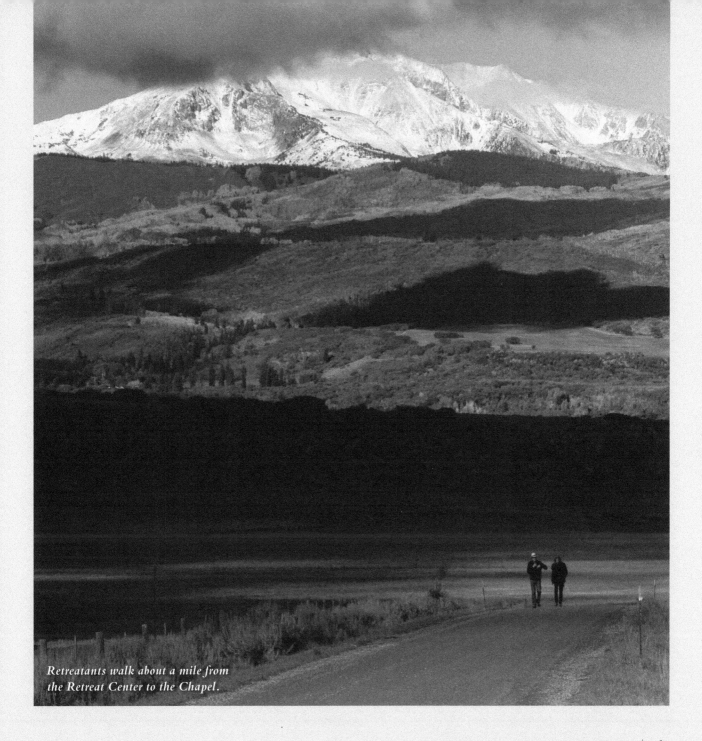

Retreatants walk about a mile from the Retreat Center to the Chapel.

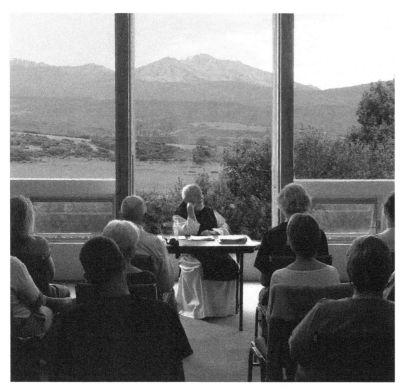

Fr. William leads a discussion at the Retreat Center.

who come for a short period of days for spiritual renewal, counseling or reflective quiet and solitude.

St. Benedict's has a truly beautiful retreat house consisting of a large central building for guests, with a dining room, reception area and meditation chapel. There are also fourteen "apartments," most of them separate buildings in the style of a hermitage, complete with washrooms and kitchens. Thus we can accommodate individuals wishing for solitude or groups wanting to share their spiritual journeys. Guests have the option of remaining in solitude, consulting with one of the monks, or attending group conferences. Once a month there is a ten-day intensive retreat for those who have at least a moderate proficiency in Centering Prayer. Occasionally there are workshops on various aspects of the spiritual life. ❖

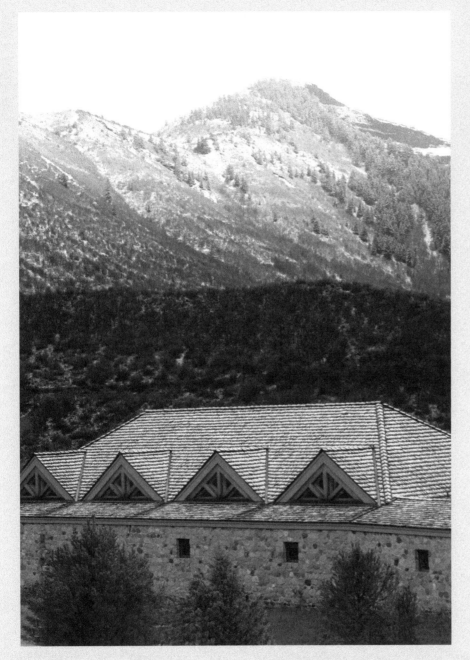

Great care and
concern are to be
shown receiving poor
people and pilgrims,
because in them most
particularly Christ
is received.

—RB 53

*Winter's first snow on the main
retreat house*

MONASTIC VOCATIONS

And the Spirit and the bride say, 'Come!' And let him who hears say, 'Come!' And let him who thirsts come; and he who wishes, let him receive the water of life freely.

—APOCALYPSE 22:17

The Bishop Dominic Marconi officiates the ordinations of Fr. Charles and Fr. Micah.

THE MONASTERY offers a place for a man—heart, mind and soul—to encounter God. Blessed to live in our majestic Rocky Mountain valley, we monks of St. Benedict's encounter God …

✤ *In the silence and solitude of Cistercian life;*

✤ *In community prayer and meditation;*

✤ *In the hours of private lectio divina;*

✤ *In the interplay of human relationships within a small community;*

✤ *In the community's work of ranching, baking, providing for guests and performing the daily chores essential to the life of the monastery;*

✤ *In the instructions of the abbot and in service to one another;*

✤ *In the nurturing of personal growth through the expression of God-given talents and theology;*

✤ *In living out the belief that our call to prayer is an effective way to bear the burdens of the Church and the world.*

Monastic life is no quick fix. It has a slower pace than life in the world, and it is directed toward a life-long commitment. Thus the discernment process is cautious, providing the seeker with time to dip a toe in the water before plunging in. Here are a few basic requirements.

❶ The candidate should be a Catholic between twenty and forty-five, unmarried, and free of family obligations or debts.

❷ He should be in good physical and mental health. The monastery must be assured that he can respond to the demands of close community living and contribute toward its need to earn its daily bread.

❸ Since monks take a vow of obedience, the candidate must be able to live with good will toward authority.

❹ The monk is vowed to a celibate life, and his need for human affection, love and friendship must be found within the monastic life according to the norms of the church's understanding of the vow of chastity.

❺ One of the monk's most challenging ascetical practices is to learn to accept his brothers as they are and to be open to their criticism of his own faults. For this reason, the person who aspires to live a monastic life must be able to let go of his own ideas and preferences when the consensus of the community is to move in a different direction.

Salve window was created by Dutch-born artist Sylvia Nicolas.

Needless to say, a warm and filial devotion to Our Lady will tend to lighten many burdens and will give our dedication a more loving generosity.

—THOMAS MERTON

The normal entrance procedure for the candidate is to arrange with the Vocation Director for a one-week visit. By working and praying with the community, the candidate gets an idea of monastic living in general and of our community in particular. If the experience proves to be mutually positive, he is invited for a return visit, during which he shares more intimately in the life of the community.

After this, the candidate is invited to enter the six-month Participant Program to live, pray and work within the community, sharing most of the obligations and privileges of the monastery. Thus, the candidate acquires a deeper insight into his suitability for the monastic life, and the community is able to make a practical judgment regarding formal entrance into the formation program for new monks.

You may feel that, though you don't want to become a monk, you would like to live a monk's life for a while. When we have space in the Participant Program, we often accept such men. For a period ranging from one to six months you may live with the community of St. Benedict's Monastery, praying, working and sharing our life. An introductory discernment visit is for a week. Following this visit, further steps in the discernment process could lead to entry into the program.

For more information, write to: Vocation Director, St. Benedict's Monastery, 1012 Monastery Road Snowmass, Colorado 81654-9399; or E-MAIL: vocations@rof.net. You can also visit our websites at www.snowmass.org and www.contemplativeprayer.net. ❖

MONKS AND PRIESTS

…there are men truly called…
to renounce even the active
Christian life…and to
become henceforth strangers
in the world, living apart,
consecrated to
silent meditation and
liturgical praise, to poverty,
manual labor, solitude,
sacred study and
spiritual discipline.

—THOMAS MERTON

Fr. Joseph blesses the palms

THE PLACE OF PRIESTS in the monastic community has changed in many ways during the centuries since St. Benedict formulated his holy rule. Originally, for the most part, monks were not priests, and St. Benedict inherited the conditions that prevailed in the monastic observances that preceded him. Thus the monasteries of Pachomius, Basil, Jerome, Cassian and Gregory had whatever priests they needed, drawn from their own ranks, in order to function as Christian communities and local churches.

However, as was inevitable, most monastic communities received into their ranks men who were already ordained to the priesthood. In general, they were allowed to function according to their priestly order with the permission of the abbot. Thus, St. Benedict makes special provision for them in his rule. Unlike the immediate predecessor to RB, the Rule of the Master, which considered priests and deacons to be "outsiders," Benedict's rule did allow priests to join his community and also allowed members of his communities to be ordained.

Priests, however, were specifically enjoined out of respect for their priesthood to be examples of humility by not expecting to outrank other monks. Even though they were given a liturgical

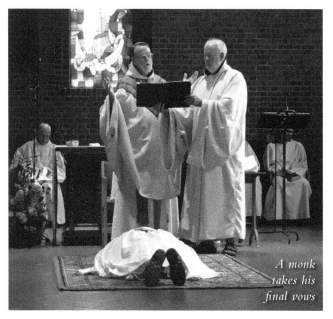

A monk takes his final vows

preference by being allowed to stand next to the abbot, in all other matters they were to take the rank they would be entitled to by reason of the date of their entry into the community. The priest could exercise his sacerdotal, or priestly, functions of blessing and celebrating Mass only with the consent of the abbot. He was ordered to be subject to the discipline of the Rule and not to make exceptions for himself. Other clerics (deacons, lectors, acolytes, porters) were "to be ranked somewhere in the middle," but only on the condition that they too promised to keep the Rule and observe monastic stability.

Do you promise obedience to me and to my successors?

—FROM THE RITE OF SOLEMN PROFESSION

The role of priests in the monastery underwent changes as the understanding of the Eucharistic liturgy changed. Increasingly during the Middle Ages the Mass was seen more and more as a sacred activity to be celebrated for its own sake—even apart from community participation. Thus by the twelfth and thirteenth centuries the phenomenon of "Mass priests" became more common. Many monks were ordained solely for the purpose of celebrating private daily Mass, even to the exclusion of other aspects of the priestly ministry. This custom continued, with minor variations, until the twentieth century. With notable exceptions, to become a monk also meant to become a priest, and ordination was often given shortly after the monk made his solemn vows, sometimes only a few days later. Studies for the priesthood

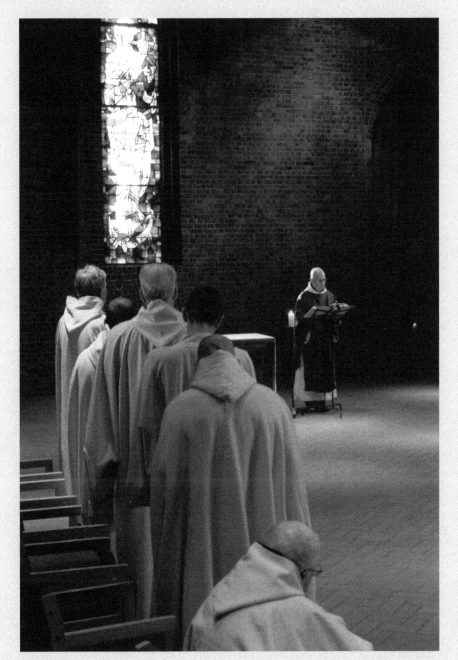

…*[the monk] was able to participate in common liturgical worship in which Christ, the Lord and Savior, was present in the midst of the monastic convocation…*

—Thomas Merton

Mass is celebrated daily.

Br. Aaron Cotter

Br. Benito Williamson

Br. Martin O'Connor

Fr. Charles Albanese, Prior

Br. Erik Keeney

Dom Joseph Boyle, Abbot

Br. Chuck Forster

Br. Raymond Roberts, Subprior

Fr. Ed Hoffman

It is not by extraordinary spiritual adventures or by dramatic and heroic exploits that the monk comes to terms with life.

—THOMAS MERTON

Br. Thomas Johnston

Dom Thomas Keating

Fr. Micah Schonberger

Br. Gabriel Lumpkin

Fr. William Meninger

Br. Neil Gomes

Good Friday Liturgy

To be worthy of the task of governing a monastery, the abbot must always remember what his title signifies and act as a superior should. He is believed to hold the place of Christ in the monastery since he is addressed by a title of Christ.

—RB 2

could begin as early as the novitiate.

Many of the larger monasteries became centers of study for preparation to the priesthood. Some of these even became the sources of today's great universities. Others still operate seminaries to prepare candidates for the priesthood even outside monastic jurisdictions. Since the Second Vatican Council there is a tendency in many Cistercian monasteries for a candidate to enter the monastery simply to become a monk, and the question of becoming a priest is put off until after solemn vows or occasionally permanently. Priests continue to be trained and ordained in monasteries (often after study "outside") but only to the degree that they are seen to be needed to serve the monastery in its capacity as a Christian community or church. This is a situation still in flux today and, as is to be expected, it varies in different houses throughout the Order. ❖

Fr. Ed Hoffman makes his solemn profession before Fr. Joseph Boyle, the abbot of St. Benedict's Monastery.

Archetype Monk

The monastery is so radically different from the "world!" Monasticism seems so much a thing of the past and so alien to technological society. The life of the monk seems on many counts to be pointless.

—Thomas Merton

The original monastery buildings on a winter day

THERE IS AN ORGANIZATION in Aspen, Colorado called the Aspen Institute for Humanistic Studies. Founded by the philosopher Mortimer Adler (1902-2001), it periodically calls together executives from businesses all over the world to meet and discuss the humanities, philosophy, religion and ethics—in other words, subjects that they as businessmen and -women are not usually exposed to. Often, as a part of the "Aspen experience," these groups make a visit to our monastery to attend our evening Vespers and Eucharistic liturgy, and to chat with the monks about our "alternative lifestyle." Most of them are not Catholic and have never before visited a monastery.

A letter received recently from an IBM executive after one such visit stated: "I am not a Catholic, possibly not even a Christian. I have never visited a monastery before and do not completely understand what I saw there or how it has affected me, but I know I am permanently changed—and for the better." Why is this? Why should a single brief visit to a monastery have such a powerful effect? Why are people so fascinated by monks and by things monastic?

One evening, Fr. Theophane (1930-2003) and I met with a group from the Aspen Institute. They seemed to be interested in every

Yet there is something of the Word that is Jesus that is spoken in the center of our beings and that reaches a recognizable expression in the monastic life.

—WILLIAM MENINGER

aspect of monastic living, and the questions were coming fast and furious long after the time allotted had expired. Taking advantage of a brief pause in the barrage of questions, Fr. Theophane remarked: "See how interested you all are in the monastic life. There is a reason for this. Something of the monk exists in every one of us." I think this is a statement of profound truth. According to Carl Jung, there

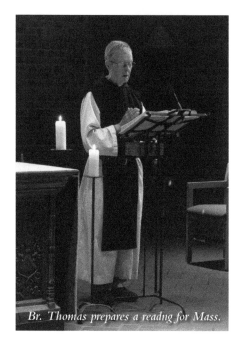

Br. Thomas prepares a readng for Mass.

exist in all of us myths or archetypes that are the forms whereby our collective unconscious represents for itself the fundamental meanings of our basic relationships. Thus there exists in each one of us something of the Man, the Woman, the King, the Evil One, the Monk, etc. It is this element of the Monk in each of us that resonates with the silence, austerity, prayer, poverty, simplicity and obedience somehow tasted in even a brief visit to a monastery.

The days are gone when the whole Church saw the monastic life as her ideal model. There are many other models, spiritualities, or theological systems that relate more and more authentically to life in this modern world. Yet monastic spirituality will always have its place. It will always speak to something that lies deep in the

Easter Sunday Procession begins before dawn with lighting the Easter fire.

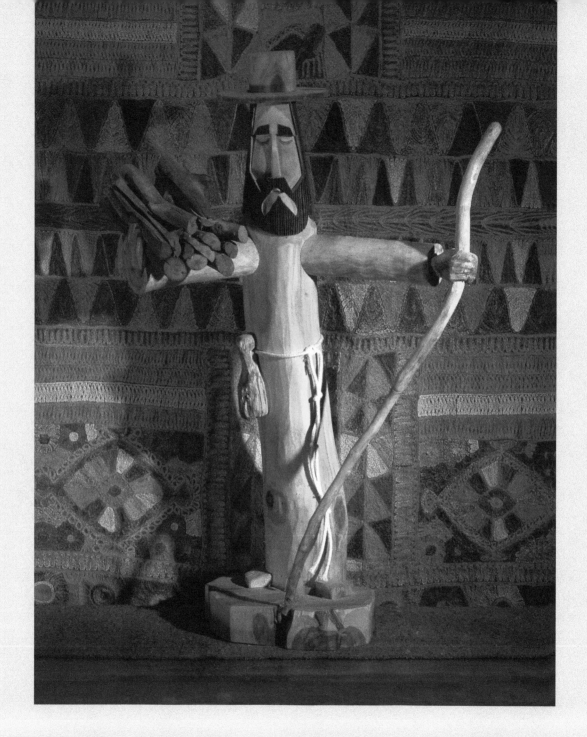

innermost being of every man and woman of every culture and religious belief. The Franciscan Liberation Theologian, Leonardo Boff, says that Jesus will not allow himself to be domesticated by any particular theological system. What Jesus tells us of God is too great to be comprehended and explained by any one form of spirituality. Jesus is the Word that must be spoken over and over again in every age, to every people, and in every culture. He is colored by every situation (so Jesus is black in Africa, yellow in Asia, white in Europe), fully expressed by none, touched upon by all.

Yet there is something of the Word that is Jesus that is spoken in the center of our beings and that reaches a recognizable expression in the monastic life. This is why monasticism is a viable witness and why encountering this witness elicits such a resonating response in the hearts of so many men and women.

For some the words "monastic" and "contemplative" are almost synonymous. To be a monk is to be a contemplative, to bear witness to the value of contemplation and to share this value with those who resonate with it and wish to support and strengthen it in themselves. This sharing is indeed a viable part of monastic spirituality, and is the reason why we Trappist monks write books and even occasionally leave our monasteries to give conferences, workshops and retreats. But above all, our witness is in the living, in the abiding communal expression of the contemplative attitude. ✤

…the full seriousness of the monastic vocation would be missed if we underestimated the sense of urgency that often drives the monk, like Lot, from the "cities of the plain" into the mountain of solitude.

—THOMAS MERTON

A "santo" from the Taos Pueblo. St. Pasquale, the patron saint of kitchens, is in front of a rug from Guatemala.

THE GOAL OF MONASTIC LIFE

He will regard all utensils and goods of the monastery as sacred vessels of the altar.

—RB 31

Br. Benito prepares the altar with chalices and host dishes.

WHAT IS THE PRIMARY GOAL of the monastic life? In the past ten years, I have interviewed scores of potential candidates for vocations. Fifty years ago, if someone came to the monastery to save his soul or to do penance for his sins, he would have been accepted without question. Today, such motives are held in suspicion—not that they are necessarily wrong, but because there are higher motivations and more authentic expressions of them that are expected today. Monastic aspirations are now expressed more in terms of loving God and desiring to seek him to the exclusion of all else, or articulated in terms of aspiring to a set of values to be pursued in a supportive community that gives witness to desiring and seeking those same values. The notion of becoming a monk because one desires heaven or fears hell is not totally absent, but it is not a dominant reason for life-choices.

People today are more human-centered than God-centered. This does not mean, as it may seem, that God takes second place to human beings. What it does mean is that God takes first place in the human rather than over the human. This is one of the basic assumptions of Liberation Theology, and it is becoming more and more an expression of the thought-patterns and motivational rationale of our young people. It is a direct result of the theological conclusions stemming from the doctrine of the Incarnation and the specific teachings of Jesus himself as expressed in the Gospels.

Where should the priority lie? What is more important, our service to one another during this life or the successful achievement of the ultimate goal of our salvation, which is eternal life with God in heaven? The two questions are, in reality, one, and the answers to both of them need not be contradictory.

Theology, like every science, has many branches. Monasticism is very much concerned with that branch called eschatology. Literally, eschatology refers to the study of the last things, specifically: death, judgment, heaven, hell. Monks are supposed to be already living the heavenly life—although not in any unrealistic sense. Monastic faith is supposed to be so strong that monks live as though the veil of faith were lifted and they find themselves constantly in God's presence. Likewise their hope is supposed to be so strong that, in a sense, they already have the fulfillment of God's presence.

This is why monastic vows are not sacraments. A sacrament is a sign. Monastic consecration is supposed to be the reality itself. In monastic poverty, monks own nothing specifically, but all that God has created is theirs. In monastic celibacy, monks do not have children or wives, but are "as angels in heaven." In monastic obedience, they find the will of God.

In the past few decades, a fascinating element of eschatology has come to the fore. Due in large part to the great scriptural work of

We must know that God regards our purity of heart and tears of compunction, not our many words.

—RB 20

A view looking north from the monastic cemetery

What is more important, our service to one another during this life or the successful achievement of the ultimate goal of our salvation, which is eternal life with God in heaven?

—WILLIAM MENINGER

scholar and humanitarian Albert Schweitzer (1875–1965), we have realized since the beginning of the twentieth century the primary place of eschatology in the New Testament. Theological speculation, influenced by this principle, has come up with some rich and wide-ranging ideas. It has been called a rediscovery of the eschatological dimension of Christian revelation. If it affects revelation, it must have significant repercussions on Christian existence. The Swiss theologian Karl Barth (1886–1968) refers to the objects of eschatology as the "ultimate realities" and claims that they are the first principles of everything. Contemporary Liberation Theologian Gustavo Gutierrez goes even further, stressing how the eschatological theme continues to grow in our understanding of God's message today. He calls eschatology the "driving force" of salvific history. For him, it is not just another branch of theology, but the very heart of living and the key to understanding Christian revelation.

The high altar at Easter

As for God,
his way is perfect.
The word of the Lord
is flawless.
He is a shield for all
who take refuge in him.

—PSALM 18

*Then will I go
to the altar of God,
my joy and
my delight.*

—PSALM 43

To understand eschatology as referring only to the last things is not enough. Extra-historical events such as the end of the world, the Second Coming, and the Last Judgment are of great import to Christians and, indeed, to all humanity, whether people believe in them or not. However, these great mysteries must be seen not as some far-off eventualities known only through faith, but as powerful incentives, divine goals, and even cosmic energetic forces calling into being our present-day activities and influencing them in the form and direction of God's eternal plan. All of our present-day events must be directed toward and worthy of "the new city of God coming down from heaven." (SEE REVELATION 21:2)

This driving impulse toward the future is grace, bestowing meaning, value, and divine direction to the present. As Gutierrez puts it, "The attraction of what is to come is the driving force of history. The action of Yahweh in history and his action at the end of history are inseparable." (*A Theology of Liberation*, NY: ORBIS, 1973, P. 164) We can only understand the real meaning of God's interventions in salvation history and in our own lives when we see that history and those lives from their eschatological perspective.

The future influences the present. The eternal now of God interfaces our past, present, and future, and reveals to us a value and significance in our activity that far exceeds the limited visions of the most farseeing prophets. History can no longer be seen as a record of the past; it is, rather, a "thrust into the future."

Monastic life receives its hope and joy from the expectation that eschatology thrusts upon it. The future hope of the world, stemming from God's promises, incarnated in the divine Word and given living force in the activity of the Holy Spirit, has its roots in the present, giving meaning to our labors, and calling forth joyous eschatological celebration.

God's ways are not our ways, yet it remains paradoxically true that the divine Word has leapt into our midst and gives us a share in his own divine life. Somehow the task we have received from Adam to carry on the work of caring for the earth is going to result, not in another tower of Babel, but in the heavenly Jerusalem. The life force motivating and informing this process from creation to New Creation is God himself manifested as the Pentecostal life-giving Spirit, living among us as the Spirit of Christ, the bond and soul of his Mystical Body, and concretely manifesting himself in every act of genuine love brought forth on this earth.

Through all of this, then, monastic spirituality is informed, inspired and motivated. The liturgical expression of monastic eschatological hope is the night office, or, as it is more aptly called, Vigils. Arising hours before dawn, monastic communities await in silent prayer, meditative readings, and psalmody the coming of Christ as symbolized by the rising sun. In faith and hope, the eschatological coming of Christ "on the clouds and in glory" (SEE MATTHEW 24:30) is anticipated and somehow grasped and realized on a daily basis. The future is thrust into the present. ❖

Besides the inspired books of the Old and New Testaments, the works read at Vigils should include explanations of Scriptures by reputable and orthodox Catholic fathers.

—RB 9

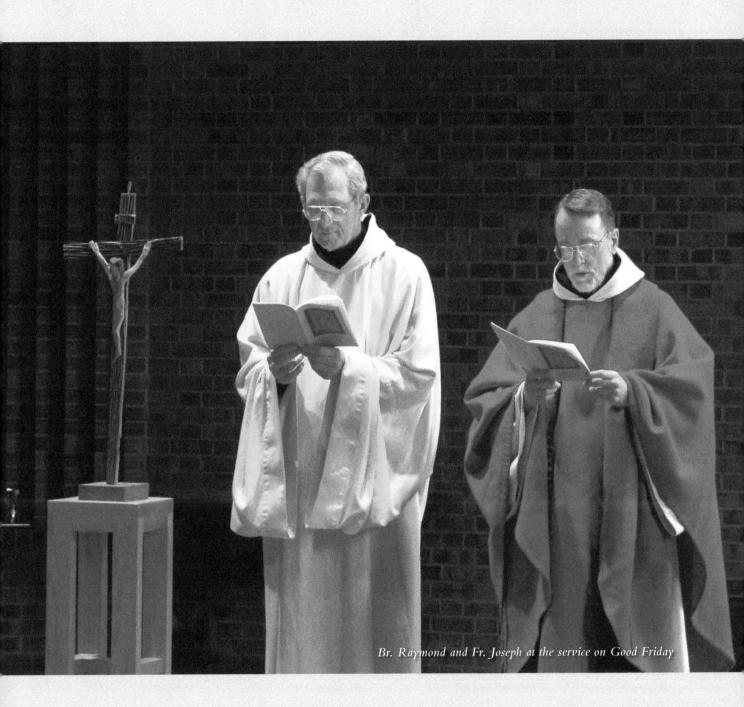

Br. Raymond and Fr. Joseph at the service on Good Friday

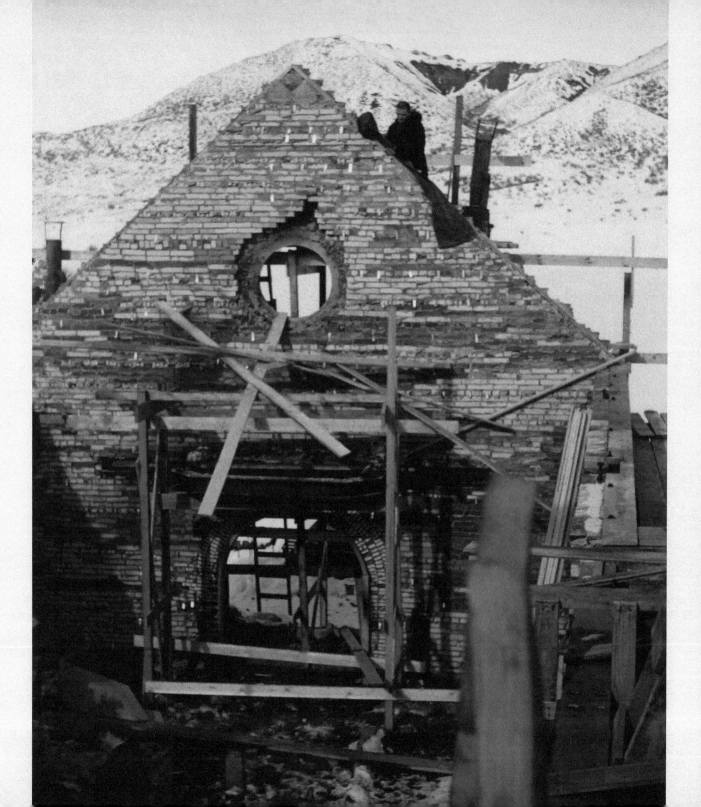

History of the Monastery

Fr. Micah Schonberger, o.c.s.o.

O Lord, you have

assigned me my portion

and my cup; you have

made my lot secure.

The boundary lines

have fallen for me

in pleasant places;

surely I have

a delightful inheritance.

—Psalm 16

The artful walls of the monastery are the work of master craftsman and bricklayer Br. Gerard, and the brothers whom he trained.

D**URING THE FRENCH REVOLUTION** and, in general, the eighteenth century, Europe cast a negative eye on Catholic religious orders. As a result, the monasteries in France were closed and confiscated, and the monks and nuns dispersed. With the dissolution of monasteries in France, survival of the Cistercian Order depended on an incredible exodus of monks from the French monastery of La Trappe (hence the name "Trappist" for our Order). Led by their novice master, Fr. Augustine de Lestrange, a group of monks, along with a group of French Cistercian nuns, sought refuge in an abandoned Carthusian monastery in Switzerland, where they followed a remarkably austere life. From Switzerland they moved from one country to another, traveling as far as Russia and, eventually, back to France, following Napoleon's defeat and exile. In 1803, while they were still in Switzerland,

Citeaux, first home of the Cistercians, Dijon, France

Lestrange sent twenty monks to North America to make a foundation. After a discouraging eleven-year struggle, these monks returned to a post-Napoleonic France less hostile to the Church.

However, one monk, Fr. Vincent de Paul Merle (1768–1853), was left behind in Halifax, Nova Scotia in May 1815. While serving as a priest in the diocese of present day Antigonish, he located a tract of land that he thought was suitable for establishing a monastery.

La Trappe Abbey • La Trappe, France

He then arranged with Fr. Lestrange, now living at the French monastery of Bellefontaine, to begin the New World foundation of Petit Clairvaux. The little community began with only five monks. Though less extreme than that of Lestrange's nomadic group, the highly ascetical life that was the hallmark of the Trappists proved too rigorous to attract many local candidates. They struggled for nearly forty years until, in 1857, the Belgian monastery of Saint Sixtus sent eighteen monks to help the surviving community work the land according to the custom of their European forerunners since medieval times.

In 1869, Petit Clairvaux was admitted into the Cistercian Order. It chose to align itself with those monasteries within the Order that observed the reforms inaugurated at the Cistercian monastery of La Trappe. By 1876 the fledgling monastery had grown sufficiently stable to become self-governing and to elect its first abbot. In 1882, the French Cistercian monastery of Bellefontaine agreed to assume the responsibility of guiding and assisting this New World community, which by then numbered forty-five monks.

On October 4, 1892, fire devoured Fr. Vincent de Paul Merle's dream. Though none of the monks was injured, the monastery lay in ruins. Determined to rebuild, the monks began the work in 1894, only to be thwarted again by fire. Discouraged, some of the monks returned to Belgium and others dispersed. By 1898 only twelve monks remained. It looked as though the history of Petit Clairvaux had come to a close.

In 1899, however, the community petitioned the Order's General Chapter (or governing body) to move the monastery from Nova Scotia to the diocese of Providence, Rhode Island. In 1900, the small community relocated on three hundred stone-strewn acres and established a new monastery called Our Lady of the Valley. There they resumed monastic life and doubled in size within about ten years. Following World War II, a tidal wave of vocations swelled the size of Catholic religious orders in the United States. By 1948, Our Lady of the Valley numbered one hundred and thirty-seven monks. As did many other monasteries in the U.S., Our Lady of the Valley made a new foundation, Our Lady of Guadalupe, in New Mexico. Two years later the old enemy, fire, lashed out again. On March 21, 1950, the Solemnity of St. Benedict, the Rhode Island monastery was destroyed, though again the monks escaped with their lives. The community of one hundred and forty monks decided to look for a new home. They found it in Spencer, Massachusetts, where they established St. Joseph's Abbey.

The community continued to grow and began making more new foundations, five between 1947 and 1960. One of those communities was established high in the Colorado Rockies in 1956. It was named St. Benedict's Monastery.

St. Joseph's Abbey • Spencer, Massachusetts

Dom Edmund Futterer

Prior to 1956, Dom Edmund Futterer, abbot of St. Joseph's Abbey, had already been considering a location on the eastern slope of the Colorado Rockies as the sight for a new monastery. At that time agriculture played the major part in Cistercian (Trappist) work and sustenance, and Dom Edmund wanted enough land to support three hundred head of cattle. However, because of an extended drought, the prospect looked discouraging on the eastern slope, and the monks began looking for land further west in Colorado's mountainous interior. In March 1954 a search party contacted a real estate agent in Grand Junction, Colorado, who directed the monks to two pieces of land, one near Snowmass and the other, called Bush Creek, further north. After looking over the Snowmass land and discovering that a road ran through the property, they passed it up and traveled north to Bush Creek. There they liked what they saw and visited the owner in Omaha, Nebraska. They were too late; another buyer had just purchased the land.

In 1955, Dom Edmund learned that land in California's Napa Valley, which he had considered for a new foundation a decade earlier, was again for sale. Stag's Leap contained one hundred and fifty acres of grape-producing land, appropriate for monastic life, as it had a ready-made industry to support it. However, the Abbey of Gethsemani in Kentucky had already purchased land for a new foundation in northern California, and the Order's General Chapter turned down Dom Edmund's request. It was reasoned that two foundations in northern California would compete for

St. Benedict's Monastery rests on nearly level ground surrounded by rough hills, and, to the west, Mt. Sopris and the Elk Mountains.

vocations. Disappointed again, Dom Edmund had to abandon the project. Today, Stag's Leap Winery produces an excellent commercial wine.

In October 1955, Dom Edmund again sent a few monks to Colorado to take another look at the Snowmass property. This time they were advised that they might be able to purchase additional land that would include the problematic road threatening the monks' privacy. (Indeed, in May 1956 they did purchase this land, securing their privacy.) The archbishop of Denver gave his blessing to the project and the Abbot General of the Order gave his approval for the foundation. Finally, the long search had ended.

St. Benedict's Monastery

St. Benedict's is home to fifteen monks who follow the sixth-century *Rule of St. Benedict.*

On February 9, 1956, four monks from St. Joseph's Abbey arrived at the new location in Snowmass and spent the first night in an old school house about a mile down the road from the property's ranch house. The next day, the feast of St. Scholastica, they moved into the ranch house, a brick structure built around 1908, and began monastic life in the Colorado Rockies. Soon three more monks arrived, including the foundation's first superior, Fr. Leo Slatterie. With three hundred and forty-three head of cattle and a 3,100-acre ranch to maintain, they had time to make only rudimentary renovations to the ranch house, preparing for the third group of monks from St. Joseph's. They arrived on April 12, bringing the number in the community to thirteen.

The community had to face two challenges that spring. All the monks were easterners who had never lived in a semiarid climate. First, they had to tackle the job of learning how to clean and use some forty miles of ditches to irrigate six hundred acres of pasture land and six hundred acres of hay fields. The monastery's elevation of nearly eight thousand feet presented the second challenge. Used to working in Trappist mode (hard), they had to learn to slow down. This was the frequent advice of Gordon LaMoy, the rancher

Construction of the Refectory (R) and the Chapel (L) begin to take shape in 1957.

Far from being a thing of the past, the monastic tree is full of young life and it is developing in new ways.

—Thomas Merton

who had sold them the major portion of land and who was hired by the monks to teach them ranching.

A major decision had to be made before beginning construction of the new monastery. The depth of topsoil was good for agriculture but too deep to support the weight of heavy buildings. They had to use pilings to support the foundation.

In May the community purchased land adjacent to the LaMoy property, adding four hundred and eighty acres to their holdings. At the same time, twelve more monks arrived from St. Joseph's Abbey, bringing the number in the community to twenty-four.

Picturesque (and back-breaking)
haying in the early years

To accommodate the growing community they converted the schoolhouse into a dormitory.

In the spring of 1958, Fr. Thomas Keating, newly appointed by Dom Edmund as superior, arrived from St. Joseph's Abbey with several other monks. On November 23 of that year, the community moved into the new monastery, now substantially complete. The next morning, Sunday, Dom Edmund sang the first mass in the chapel.

Seeking an additional industry to support the community, the monks started a candy business in the spring of 1959. It was short-lived due to an unanticipated phenomenon: made at the monastery's high elevation, the hard candy cracked when it reached lower elevations. Not to be deterred, the community decided on a new business venture of maintaining a cow-calf operation. Unfortunately, this proved too much for the monks. From the proceeds of the cattle sale, they bought ten thousand chickens and built two Quonset huts to house them. In 1967, they began selling the eggs to local restaurants. The industry was a success and helped to support the community for eighteen years. It is ironic that so much time, energy and expense had gone into securing a large ranch to support a cattle operation.

In 1961, the monks at the motherhouse in Massachusetts elected Fr. Thomas as their abbot, and he had to return to St. Joseph's Abbey. As abbot of the Spencer community, he appointed their prior, Fr. Joachim Viens, to take his place as superior of St. Benedict's. Fr. Joachim served the community as superior until 1967, when Fr. Michael Abdo was appointed. By 1970, the Snowmass community had grown large and stable enough for the monastery to become an abbey in its own right, independent from the jurisdiction of their motherhouse, the founding monastery in Massachusetts. On March 31st of that year, Fr. Michael Abdo was elected the first abbot of St. Benedict's Abbey.

During the years following Vatican II (1962–1965), religious life in the United States became unsettled, and St. Benedict's, like most other religious houses, experienced a large-scale exodus of members. By 1978 there were only seven left in the community. They bonded together with dedication and kept their monastic life and witness alive through the difficult years of the 1970s, waiting for the Holy Spirit's call to bring new members.

Following the reforms of Vatican II, the Order modified its traditional emphasis on asceticism in favor of a more contemplative way of life, and permission was given for the monks to move from the traditional common dormitory into private rooms. In 1976, the community decided to build a new dorm wing of fifteen rooms—they kept alive their hope for new members—to give the monks more personal privacy. Generous benefactors made the project possible, and construction on the new dorm wing was completed late that year.

The need for new members was acute, and Dom Ambrose Southy, the Abbot General of the Order, encouraged St. Joseph's Abbey to loan them personnel. However, meeting its own needs following Vatican II presented St. Joseph's with a manpower challenge as well, and it was unable to send anyone. Nevertheless, perseverance paid off. In time St. Joseph's did send some monks, and a few of them, finding life in the Rockies at St. Benedict's to their liking, transferred to the struggling community.

Monastic life did not regain its popularity following the exodus after Vatican II, and the community created a new vocational program both to help with the work and to give men a chance to experience

Bodily discipline and asceticism are essential to a serious monastic life...

—THOMAS MERTON

St. Benedict's Monastery Library

Cistercian life without having to make a permanent commitment. The Participant Program, begun in 1983, served this twofold purpose. It has turned out to be a success and continues to the present day, drawing men into the community for longer commitments, including three who went on to make solemn profession.

Encouraged by this stirring of new life, the community decided to convert the old dorm area into individual rooms. In August 1981 they completed the first stage of four rooms. That summer they also built a greenhouse attached to one of the Quonsets, enabling the monks to raise some of their own food as they strove to embrace the monastic tradition of providing, as far as possible, for their own needs.

During the 1970s and 1980s, the community welcomed teachers from other religious traditions. One such teacher, Maesumi Roshi, gave a workshop on the Buddhist contemplative tradition. It was a way of responding to Pope Paul VI's call to Catholic monastic communities to engage in ecumenical dialogue with Eastern religious traditions.

During the long winters the community found it difficult to celebrate early morning Vigils in the unheated church. In the autumn of 1982 they decided to insulate the church and install doors to separate it from the unheated cloister hallway. The project

called for putting stucco over the original brickwork on the outside of the church. It was a trade off between aesthetics and comfort.

In 1984, having returned to St. Benedict's after serving as abbot of St. Joseph's for twenty years, Fr. Thomas Keating began an ecumenical dialogue group called the Snowmass Conference. The experiment, which included representatives from Native American, Buddhist, Hindu, Muslim, Eastern Orthodox, and Protestant traditions, continued to meet annually for the next eleven years.

Fr. Thomas Keating (L) and Fr. William Meininger (R)

During these post-Vatican II years of the Catholic Church's ecumenical thrust, Fr. William Meninger, a monk of St. Joseph's Abbey, began giving retreats based on a fourteenth-century, anonymous treatise on contemplative prayer. *The Cloud of Unknowing* presents a method for entering into deep, mystical prayer. Building on Fr. William's work, Fr. Thomas and another Spencer monk, Fr. M. Basil Pennington, began giving retreats based on this model of silent, contemplative prayer. The objective was to reclaim the tradition of contemplative prayer for Western Christianity. Because of Fr. Thomas' work in establishing Contemplative Outreach, an organization to promote a method of contemplative prayer known as Centering Prayer, St. Benedict's Monastery today serves as spiritual home for the international Centering Prayer movement, begun by these three contemplative monks.

The entrance to the refectory

Dom Joseph Boyle

During the 1980s, the monastery's egg industry began to experience falling prices, and when in 1984 their industry's future seemed bleak, the monks decided to phase it out and replace it with a small bakery for making cookies. On May 9, 1986, they began selling cookies to local supermarkets.

In April 1985, after serving the community as superior for eighteen years, Fr. Michael stepped down as abbot, and on May 29 the community elected Fr. Joseph Boyle. On July 11, the Solemnity of St. Benedict, Auxiliary Bishop Dominic Marconi of Newark, New Jersey, bestowed the Church's official blessing on the community's new abbot.

Fire, the old archenemy, struck again on April 22, 1986. The spring cleaning of irrigation ditches included the burning of brush that had accumulated over the winter. One such burning went out of control for two hours, consuming a hay shed and a delivery truck and damaging a tractor.

By October of that year, work to convert the old dorm into individual rooms was complete, and the small community had room to accommodate twenty-five people. In the autumn of 1987 this growing community began meeting with Diane Fassel, a professional group facilitator, in order to improve the monks' skills in communicating with one another. The venture proved to be a blessing, and the community has continued the meetings for eighteen years.

St. Aelred Hermitage at the Retreat Center

On May 31, 1991, the monks reelected Fr. Joseph as their abbot, and in July, addressing their need for new retreat facilities, they met for the first time with architects from the Aspen firm of Conger and Fuller. Plans were drawn up, and fund raising began. Through the generosity of benefactors, the monks, unable themselves to construct the new facilities, hired a contractor, and construction got underway. On October 18, 1992, the monks gathered with benefactors and held the traditional ground breaking and blessing ceremony. On February 12, 1993, when the builders finished the framework for the top of the first building, the community and construction crew celebrated a traditional "topping off" party.

The next year, concerned about the pace of housing and commercial development in the area, the monks joined with three other adjacent large landowners to insure protection from developers. They attempted an agreement to keep their combined 10,000 or more acres rural and agricultural. Due to inevitable complexities, ten years of legal negotiations ended with no resolution.

After four years of fund raising and construction, the new retreat house became a reality, and on July 11, 1995, it was consecrated. In perfect weather, about ninety invited donors helped to celebrate the conclusion of what had been thirty years of discussions and planning for a new facility. The last four years had made the new retreat house a reality. It was a successful project in more ways than one. The effort created a retreat house, which caught the attention of the American Institute of Architects which, in 1996, singled it out for excellence in religious architecture that year.

In 1996, the monks were able to celebrate Fr. Thomas' fiftieth anniversary of profession, an event to which their motherhouse, St. Joseph's Abbey, sent two monks to represent the community he had led for twenty years.

In 1997, the community reelected Fr. Joseph as abbot and stipulated that he remain in that office indefinitely rather than for the usual term of six years. This decision was not only a vote of confidence in his effective leadership, but also an expression of the monks' love and respect for him personally.

The monks had one more pressing issue to address. As a young community, they had not experienced a pressing need for rooms to accommodate the sick and elderly. An older community now, the time had come to provide assisted living quarters. They hired two of the architects who had worked on the retreat house and began a fund-raising campaign. Friends again responded generously. The new wing took a year of noisy, dust-filled construction to build, but shortly before Christmas 2000 it was ready for occupancy.

In October 1998, during one of its communications workshops

The monk is valuable to the world precisely in so far as he is not part of it, and hence it is futile to try to make him acceptable by giving him a place of honor in it.

—THOMAS MERTON

Br. Benito Williamson
Fr. Charles Albanese
Fr. Micah Schonberger

with Diane Fassel, the community addressed the task of creating a vision statement. Reflecting on their own lives and the monastery's purpose, they drew up the following: "Through daily life in our Cistercian community, we aspire to be transformed in mind and heart by embodying Christ Jesus in ways appropriate to our times."

In the opening years of the twenty-first century, the community celebrated two more fiftieth anniversaries; in 2003 Br. Benito Williamson, and in 2004 Br. John Collins celebrated fifty years of vows in the monastic life. At the same time, the community experienced the need for more priests since no monk had been ordained for more than thirty years, and only three priests remained in its ranks. In May 2004 they called two brothers to the priesthood. On July 11, 2005, exactly twenty years after he had blessed Fr. Joseph as abbot, Bishop Dominic Marconi ordained Brothers Charles Albanese and Micah Schonberger to the priesthood. The community again looks to the future with faith in God's providence and an openness to embrace his will. ✣

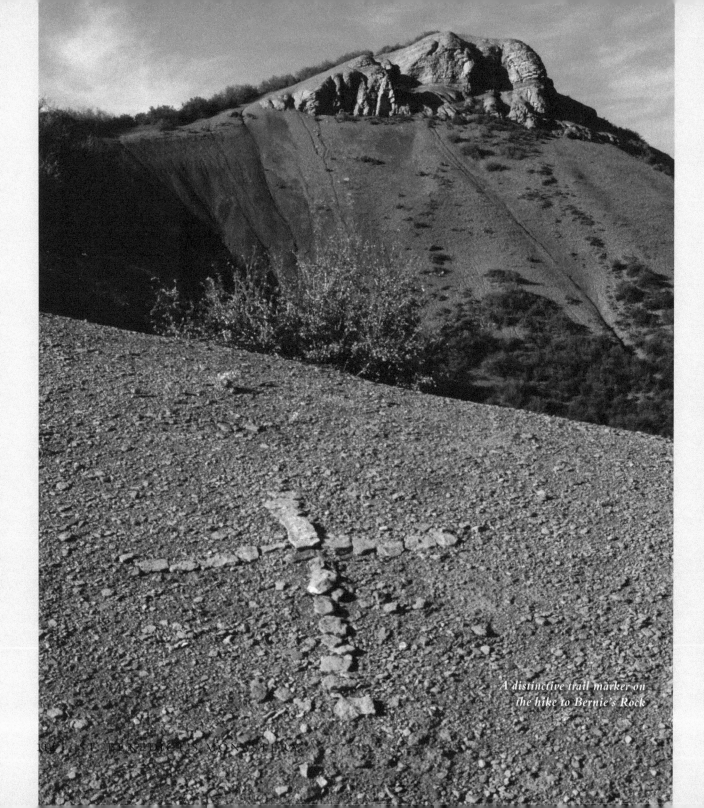

A distinctive trail marker on the hike to Bernie's Rock

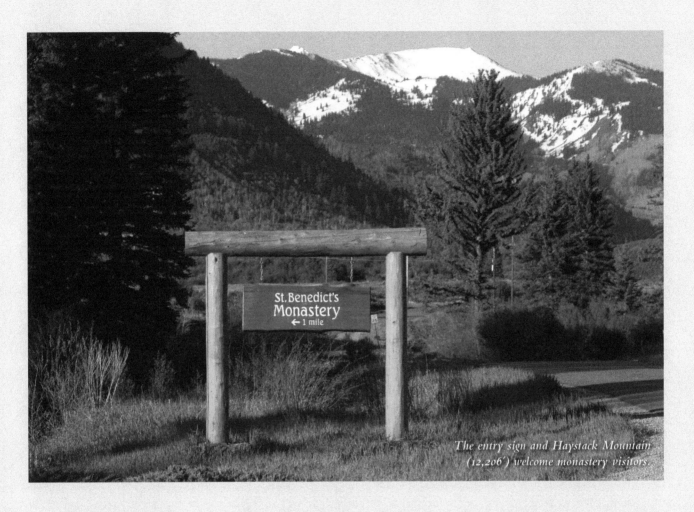

The entry sign and Haystack Mountain (12,206´) welcome monastery visitors.

Thou wilt bring them in and plant them on Thy own mountain

The place, O Lord, which Thou hast made for Thy abode

The sanctuary, O Lord, which Thy hands have established.

—EXODUS 15:17

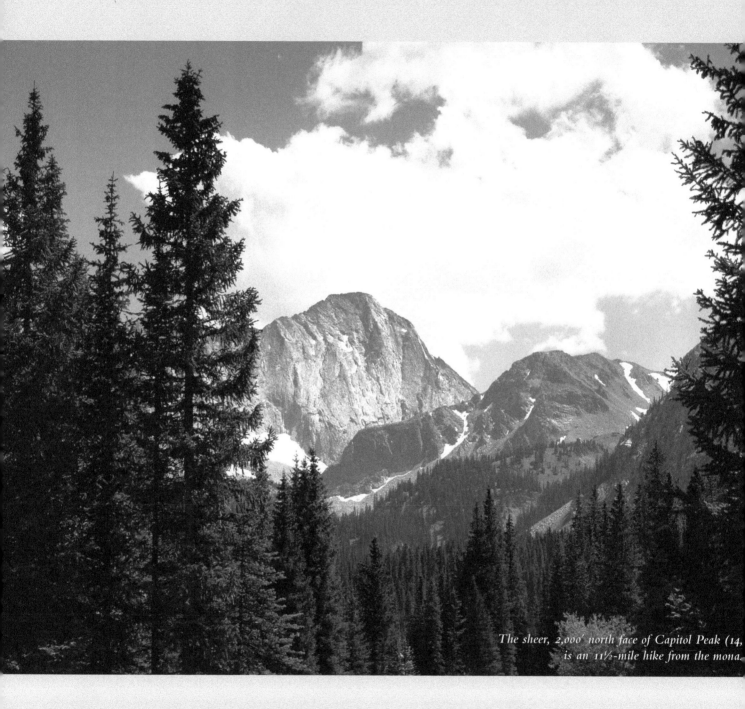

The sheer, 2,000' north face of Capitol Peak (14,
is an 11½-mile hike from the mona

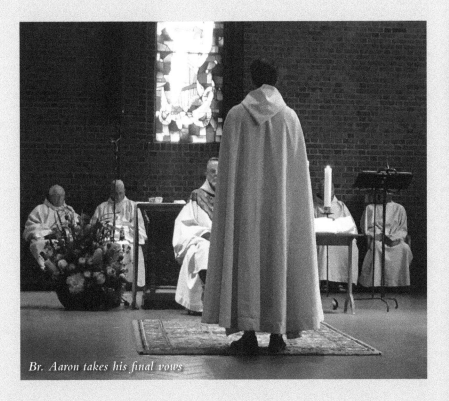

Br. Aaron takes his final vows

The south cloister

To come face to face with
the mystery of the monastic vocation
and to grapple with it
is a profound experience.

—THOMAS MERTON

Br. Erik prepares asparagus

The ranch house was the monastery while the brothers were building the present structure.

*When someone enters St. Benedict's Monastery at Snowmass
he intends to live and die in this one mountain valley, in this one community
with its special graces, advantages, problems and limitations.*

—THOMAS MERTON

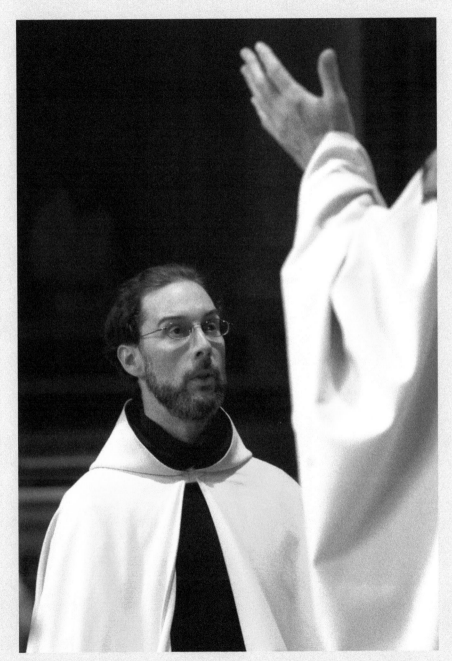

It is by suffering
in silence
that we come to know
the deep inner joy
that silence alone
can open up to the heart
that seeks God.

—THOMAS MERTON

Br. Aaron receives a blessing
during his final vows.

CONFORMITY TO CHRIST

FR. JOSEPH BOYLE, O.C.S.O.

"LORD JESUS, who are you and who am I?" I often use this question to focus myself as I enter into quiet prayer. Just who is this Christ that we seek to be conformed to? The mystery of Christ is so vast and rich that no line of thought can do it justice. Yet, key for me is that Jesus Christ was and is the place of God's presence among us: Emanuel-God with us.

The Dutch theologian Eduard Schillebeeckx referred to Christ as "the sacrament of encounter with God."

When I reflect on the theme "Cistercian Grace Today: Conformity To Christ" it seems to me that we are called individually and collectively as a community to be the sacrament of encounter with God—in union with Christ to be a place of God's presence in the world.

This affects all aspects of our life.

In worship we are united with Christ, as all creation comes to consciousness in us and is able to praise and celebrate the Creator. We pray the very psalms that Christ prayed, we join Him in His Eucharistic prayer to the Father. In Snowmass, partly because of the small size of our community, our liturgy does not have the splendor of liturgies in our larger communities. Nonetheless, it has

Bishop Casey, presents a chalice and paten to the newly ordained Fr. Micah Schonberger (L) and Fr. Charles Albanese (R).

a simple grace to it, the prayer is real, and Christ's presence fills the silences. Our singing is sometimes accompanied by the singing of the coyotes and our chapel's clear glass windows let in the grandeur and beauty of the nature surrounding us.

In spiritual reading and quiet prayer we grow in our consciousness of our union with Christ and open ourselves to his spirit working in us—the spirit that transforms us into the image Christ.

In our Cistercian community relationships we become the presence of Christ for one another. In our caring for and being cared for, in our forgiving and being forgiven, the life of Christ flows through us. "Seniors love the juniors, juniors respect your seniors." In practicing this admonition from St. Benedict we offer to society an example that can heal the increasing division between generations in our modern world. At Snowmass, in our respect for the unique process of growth in Christ to which each member of the community is committed, we strive to nurture a freedom in each member that will be conducive to a mature responsibility as a Cistercian monk for the vitality and Christ-centerdness of the communities direction

Cistercians are also the presence of Christ in our relationship with the full body of Christ, which we embrace and support with our loving prayer and which we receive with hospitality, receiving them as Christ, and receiving them as Christ would receive them. In our hospitality Cistercian monasteries provide an environment for guests and retreatants to be drawn into the presence of God and into encounter with God. It seems to me that is why so many people are coming to our monasteries for retreat and liturgy these days. Hopefully these people carry the peace and love they find back to their own communities.

We also hope to be the presence of God for our neighbors. I think of our brothers at Atlas and the deep bond they had with their neighbors in that farm community, a bond so deep that the brothers chose to stay in that place with those neighbors even if it were to mean their deaths. As I understand it they did not feel the need to preach explicitly about Jesus, sufficient if the people around them could experience Christ's love through them.

Cistercians seek to be the place of Christ's presence in our relationship with the environment where our farms, ranches, orchards, and lands are stewarded with deep respect for the Creator and for His designs, continuing God's care for the world—His care for His creation. We are becoming more reflexively or self-consciously aware of this stewardship today. The truth is that this stewardship of the land has always been a part of the Cistercian tradition where our monasteries were models for good stewardship. Today we have a heightened sensitivity for how our actions are affecting the well-being and future of our human family and our whole planet. This stewardship in partnership with the Creator also shapes our response to the prevailing ethos of so many today, especially in the wealthier countries, namely consumerism: the continual purchase of new products in a throwaway culture. Our

Our singing is sometimes accompanied by the singing of the coyotes and our chapel's clear glass windows let in the grandeur and beauty of the nature surrounding us.

—JOSEPH BOYLE

stewardship hopefully exemplifies a healthy alternative for living simply on the land.

"Lord Jesus, who are you and who am I?" This question normally serves to focus and silence my inner being, but once in an age an answer emerges to the question—from wherever it is in a person that such answers come. On one particular occasion when I had just become Abbot and was wondering what I could do to bring back the spirit of the "good old days," I was sitting quietly while this question was echoing in the back of my mind and suddenly I heard the text of Revelation, "Behold, I am He who makes all things new." I had to laugh because I was focused on bringing back the old and Christ was turning me a full 180 degrees around so that with Him I could face the new. Of course we reverently carry the core of our tradition into the new with us, but still the challenge of being with and in Christ as He makes all things new is what we face today.

To conform to Christ in this way—being the place of God's presence—requires that we more and more take on the mind and heart of Christ; Christ's way of loving. This we do both individually and as a community.

Individually to do this requires that we be deeply nourished by lectio and prayer in all of its forms, but especially I would underline (at least from my experience and that of my community) the transformation that comes from quiet, wordless contemplative prayer. I see in this a connection with Jesus going off alone to

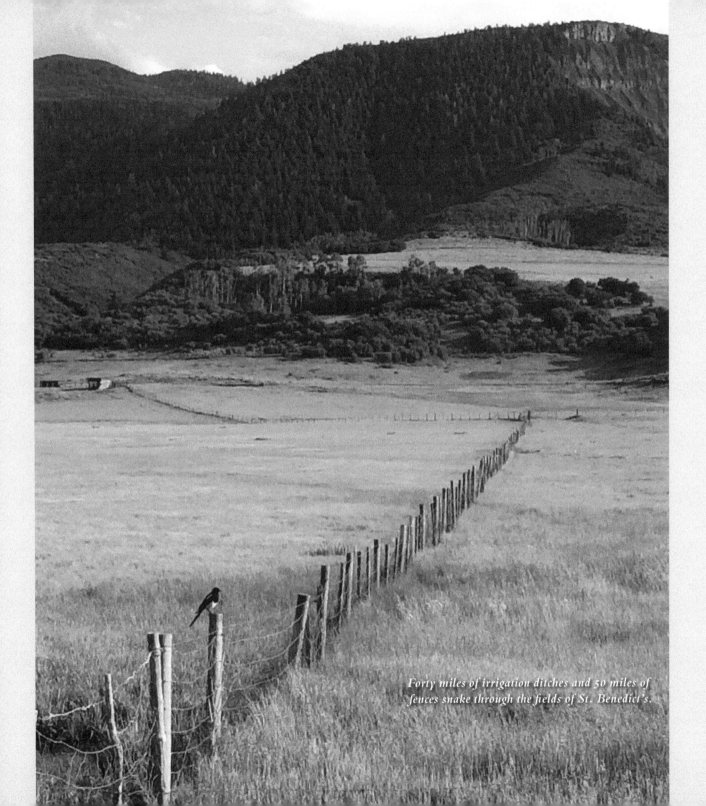

Forty miles of irrigation ditches and 50 miles of fences snake through the fields of St. Benedict's.

pray at night to be nourished at the fountain of Divine Union. Sometimes, in the early morning hours, I find my consciousness being focused by the prayerful question: "Lord, what shape do you want to take in me today."

Collectively to take on the mind and heart of Christ requires not only that the individuals in the community be deeply committed to their own process of transformation in Christ, but also that the community itself be able to discern together what is the special and particular presence of Christ we are to be in the world today in our unique situations. Being mindful of St. Benedict's phrase that God often reveals what is better to the younger, it is so important that we learn to listen to one another, each and every one in the community, pray over these things, and discern together on how we will live this Christ-life in our concrete, day to day situations. I see the work that many of our communities are doing to improve the communication skills among the members as a helpful tool in this process of working together to know and live the mind and heart of Christ.

In our time of rapid and radical social and cultural change this personal transformation and communal listening and discerning are especially necessary. To be the presence of God in the world today in conformity with Christ is a deep challenge to each of us and each one of our communities. It is critical today to be in touch with and reflect what is essential in a word where the essential is often lost sight of and where materialism and moral confusion

In our hospitality Cistercian monasteries provide an environment for guests and retreatants to be drawn into the presence of God and into encounter with God.

— JOSEPH BOYLE

are wreaking havoc. This can only flow from an ever-deeper communion with Christ.

We are blessed at this Chapter to be gathered here at Lourdes, the place where our Mother Mary spoke to St. Bernadette Soubirous a century and a half ago, a place where heaven and earth met, a place where God's healing presence touches so many. Hopefully our communities also are places where heaven and earth touch and God's healing presence comes alive in us and through us. Then are we truly conformed to His Christ, our Emmanuel. ❖

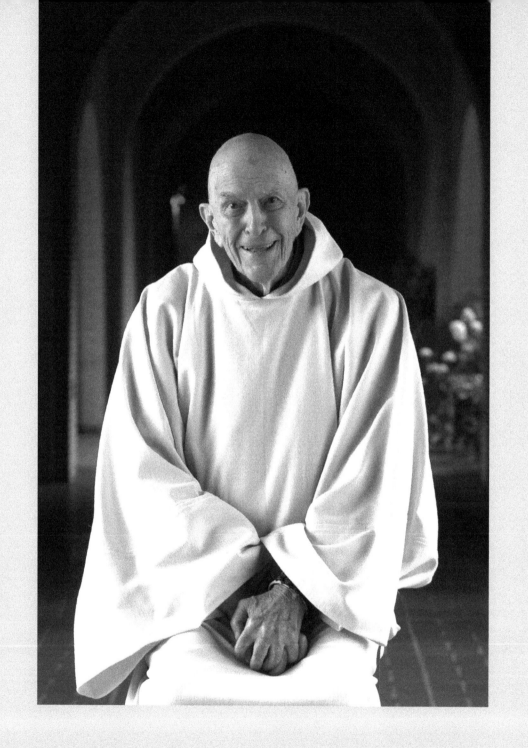

INTIMACY WITH CHRIST

FR. THOMAS KEATING, O.C.S.O.

CENTERING PRAYER is sometimes accused of falling short of true intimacy with Christ. What is meant by "true intimacy?"

Ordinarily we think of prayer as thoughts or feelings expressed in words. Contemplative prayer, the pure gift of God, is the opening of mind and heart—our whole being—to the Divine Presence within us, beyond thinking, conversing, and even consciousness itself.

Centering Prayer is a method that prepares our faculties to awaken to the gift of contemplation. It leads to an intimate relationship with Christ that is beyond words and moves into communion with him both in daily prayer and action. Centering Prayer is Christo-centric and consistent with the Christian mystical interpretation of the Gospel. Through the work of the Holy Spirit, Centering Prayer leads to a deeper intimacy with Christ.

Jesus invites us to learn this kind of prayer in his Discourse at the Last Supper: "I do not pray for them alone (those at the supper). I also pray for those who through their preaching will believe in me. All are to be one; just as you Father are in me and I am in you, so they too are to become one in us." And a little later: "The glory you have bestowed on me, I have bestowed on them, that they may

Dom Thomas Keating is a Trappist monk and priest, former superior of St. Benedict's Monastery, former Abbot of St. Joseph's Abbey, friend of the Dalai Lama, and one of the architects of Centering Prayer.

be one as we are one—I in them and you in me. Thus their oneness will be perfected...*May the love with which you love me dwell in them as I dwell in them myself.*" (JOHN 17:20-26)

This is the teaching that Centering Prayer proposes, following the whole Christian contemplative tradition, and brought into dialogue with contemporary psychological, anthropological. and neurological discoveries, as well as with the wisdom teachings of other religious traditions.

In Catholic theology, Jesus is not just a human being possessing a complete human nature. He is the Word made flesh, the Son of God, who in his divine nature assumed the historical humanity of Jesus. It is through the person of Jesus, the Divine Human Being, that we are drawn to experience the Eternal Word of God, not just through abstract theological formulas, but directly.

At Jesus' baptism in the Jordan, the Father's voice rang out saying, "This is my beloved Son ... Listen to him." This listening points to prayer as an intimate relationship with God. As listening deepens, so does the relationship with God, which gradually matures over time until we become one with him. This is the thrust of the practice of Lectio Divina: first to know Jesus in his humanity and historical life; then to know him in his passion, death, and resurrection; then to know Jesus in his resurrection; and finally to know him in his Ascension and risen life in the Trinity.

The practices of Centering Prayer and Lectio Divina open us to

The principal effects of Centering Prayer are experienced in daily life, not in the period of Centering Prayer itself.

—THOMAS KEATING

*Contemplative Prayer
is the opening
of mind and heart
—our whole being—
to God,
the Ultimate Mystery,
beyond thoughts,
words, and
emotions.*

—Thomas Keating

new levels of responding to the Spirit of God within. This growing relationship may require different responses from us as each level unfolds. In other words, the focus of each level is distinct and produces different results. To grow in divine love, through the earlier stages of relationship, is to experience a deeper knowledge and love of Christ. They change one's perspective not only of God but of all reality.

Centering Prayer is not meant to replace other kinds of prayers. Rather it casts a new light and depth of meaning on them. Centering Prayer embraces the unitive stage of Lectio Divina, as do all Christian prayer practices that encourage complete surrender to Christ.

The source of Centering Prayer is the Divine Indwelling, where one is responding to the call of the Holy Spirit to consent to the Divine Presence and action within oneself. Through the continuing practice of Centering Prayer, we experience a deepening commitment to the needs and rights of each member of the human family and an increasing respect for the interdependence and oneness of all creation.

As we move from conversation to communion with God's human and divine nature, we experience the divine intimacy as it was practiced in the first few centuries and preserved in the Christian contemplative tradition both in the West and in the Eastern Orthodoxy. The contemplative life, already present within us through the Divine Indwelling, awaits our consent.

—*Contemplative Outreach News* | June 2016

The life-size crucifix in the refectory was created by Br. Benedict Grant in 1985.

THE RULE OF ST. BENEDICT

The Rule of St. Benedict is simply an application of the Gospel counsels and commands of Christ to the monastic way of life. The Observances and Customs of the Cistercians seek to interpret and apply the Rule in greater detail.

—THOMAS MERTON

THE FIRST WORD of Benedict's Rule is, "Listen," and what's more, "Listen carefully." The admonition is to listen to God, of course, but also to abide by the "master's instructions" and "to attend to them with the ear of the heart." It is through obedience to the will of God and the teachings of the master that one comes to renounce one's own will. Benedict quotes scripture in the Prologue (and throughout the rule) many times to both admonish and encourage.

CHAPTER 1 | *The Kinds of Monks*

The first chapter of the Rule is Benedict's description of four types of monks. His purpose is to draw attention to the acceptable type, the cenobite, who leads a stable life in a community under a rule and an abbot.

CHAPTER 2 | *Qualities of the Abbot*

The abbot is believed to hold the place of Christ in the monastery. He is advised to rule not so much by decree and command as by example, patience and understanding.

CHAPTER 3 | *Summoning the Brothers for Counsel*

In important matters, the abbot calls the community together, explains the business and listens to the advice of the brothers. The final decision is the abbot's.

CHAPTER 4 | *The Tools for Good Works*

"Tools," in this instance, are standards of behavior aimed at disciplining oneself and humbly interacting with others in the community. Admonitions from scripture are bountiful.

CHAPTER 5 | *Obedience*

This quality is clearly very important to Benedict and could be called the foundation upon which his Rule rests. It is the source of humility and service and is to be given not only to superiors, but to brothers as well. It should be given willingly and not halfheartedly.

CHAPTER 6 | *Restraint of Speech*

Here is the core teaching on silence for which monastic tradition is known. In general, restraint is urged. In the community, one speaks by permission.

CHAPTER 7 | *Humility*

This much studied Chapter is perhaps the heart of the rule.

Benedict outlines twelve steps of humility: 1. Live ever in the presence of God, 2. Seek not your own will or desires, 3. Be obedient to superiors, 4. Endure obedience under unpleasant conditions with fortitude, 5. Do not hide a troubled heart from the abbot, 6. Be content with insignificant tasks, 7. Be convinced in your heart that you are of small importance, 8. Do only what is endorsed by the rule of the monastery and the example of the superiors, 9. Remain silent, 10. Avoid easy laughter, 11. Speak gently, modestly and quietly, and 12. Manifest humility in manner and posture.

CHAPTER 8 – CHAPTER 18

These chapters outline the structures and times for the Divine Office, the set times for community prayer. Specific Psalms are suggested for each of the Hours.

CHAPTER 19 | *The Discipline of Psalmody*

Psalms are to be sung reverently.

CHAPTER 20 | *Reverence in Prayer*

Pray with devotion and humility, purity of heart and honest emotion. Prayer in community is to be brief.

CHAPTER 21 | *The Deans of the Monastery*

In very large monasteries, deans are appointed to supervise groups of ten brothers. They work closely with the abbot in supervising their groups.

CHAPTER 22, | *Sleeping Arrangements*

Monks sleep in separate beds, all in one place, in their clothing and belts (knives should be removed to avoid accidental injuries).

CHAPTER 23-28 | *Brothers who are Excommunicated*

These chapters cover the treatment of brothers who are excommunicated from the community. The extent of this punishment depends on the nature of the misdeed. Other brothers may not associate with the miscreant (a kind of shunning), and the abbot is expected to make a special effort to return these brothers to the fold. If the offending brother refuses to amend his ways, he may be removed from the community altogether.

OWNERSHIP

Individual brothers are to have no personal possessions. Everything the brother needs is provided by the monastery and held in common.

—RB 33

This icon the Virgin of the Sweet Kiss was "written" for St. Benedict's Monastery by a monk from a monastery on Mount Athos in Greece..

CHAPTER 35 | *Kitchen Servers of the Week*

This Chapter outlines duties in the kitchen. No brother should be excused from this.

CHAPTER 36 | *The Sick Brothers*

Care of the sick is very important. They should be housed in a separate room, and dietary regulations may be relaxed for them.

CHAPTER 37 | *The Elderly and Children*

Consideration is to be made for the weakness of elderly members and children.

CHAPTER 38 | *The Reader for the Week*

In Benedict's Rule, meals are always accompanied by reading. All are silent and attentive to the reading. Brothers read and sing according to ability, not seniority.

CHAPTER 39 | *The Proper Amount of Food*

Two kinds of cooked food are recommended with the possible addition of fresh fruit or vegetables and bread (one pound for the day!). Except for the sick, all are to abstain from the meat of any four-footed animal.

CHAPTER 40 | *The Proper Amount of Drink*

Except for the sick, the brothers should not receive more than half a bottle of wine a day. Personal restraint is encouraged.

CHAPTER 41 | *The Times for the Brother's Meals*

This Chapter sets out the times of day for meals. These times vary with seasonal observances.

CHAPTER 42 | *Silence after Compline*

Silence is recommended as a general rule, but it is to be strictly observed at night after the Office of Compline. This Chapter also suggests a reading attended by the brothers before the final Office.

CHAPTER 43 | *Tardiness in Choir or at Meals*

Here, punishments for lateness at meals or the Divine Office are specified.

CHAPTER 44 | *Satisfaction by the Excommunicated*

In this Chapter, Benedict suggests the manner in which those accused of serious faults are to be returned to the community.

CHAPTER 45 | *Mistakes in the Oratory*

Anyone who makes a mistake during the singing of an Office must make satisfaction before the community.

CHAPTER 46 | *Faults Committed in Other Matters*

Anyone who commits a fault (breaks or loses something, ignores the customs of the house, etc.) is to come forward on his own and make satisfaction before the community. If the reason for the mistake lies in a personal problem, the brother may make it known to the abbot or a spiritual elder.

CHAPTER 47 | *Announcing the Hours for the Work of God (The Divine Office)*

Times for the Divine Office should be clearly made known to all. Those who read or sing should do so humbly, seriously and reverently.

CHAPTER 48 | *Daily Manual Labor*

All the brothers should have specified times for manual labor and for prayerful reading. These times and tasks will vary according to the locale and season.

CHAPTER 49 | *Observance of Lent*

Benedict advises that for the monk his entire life should be one continuous Lent. Since not all have the strength for this, let the brothers increase their austerity beyond the usual practice during the season. No one is to undertake any action, though, without the express permission of the abbot.

CHAPTER 50 | *Brothers Working Away, or Traveling*

Those whose work is at a distance from the house should observe the hours of the Office where they find themselves. Likewise, those traveling are to continue this practice as best they can.

CHAPTER 51 | *Brothers on a Short Journey*

A brother sent on a short, one-day journey must not eat while outside the monastery, even if invited.

CHAPTER 52 | *The Oratory of the Monastery*

The Oratory, or Chapel, should be respected as such and not be used for any other purpose. Silence is to be maintained. Brothers may enter the Oratory for private prayer.

CHAPTER 53 | *The Reception of Guests*

All guests are "to be welcomed as Christ." Guests are received with prayer and generosity with especial care afforded the poor and pilgrims.

We believe that for each monk a cowl and a tunic will suffice in temperate regions.

—RB 55

CHAPTER 54 | *Letters or Gifts for Monks*

Monks are not allowed to receive letters or exchange gifts with those inside or outside the monastery unless it is approved by the abbot.

CHAPTER 55 | *The Clothing and Footwear of the Brothers*

Clothing depends on local conditions and should be made of material available locally at reasonable cost. It should fit well and be in good repair. In addition, this chapter specifies a mat, blanket and pillow for sleeping and extra clothing for traveling.

CHAPTER 56 | *The Abbot's Table*

The abbot generally eats with guests, but may invite some of the brothers if no guests are present.

CHAPTER 57 | *The Artisans of the Monastery*

Craftsmen in the monastery may practice their arts but with humility.

CHAPTER 58 | *The Procedure for Receiving Brothers*

Entrance to the monastery should not be easy. A senior adept at caring for new arrivals supervises the progress of the novice, and the rigors of monastic life must be made plain. After an appropriate time, the novice comes before the whole community promising stability, fidelity to monastic life and obedience. The new entrant relinquishes any personal possessions and is clothed in the habit of the monastery.

Nobles and the poor may offer their sons to the community, but with the promise that they will not support the boy with income or possessions of any kind.

PORTER OF THE
MONASTERY

*The porter of the
monastery is a kind of
gatekeeper and greets
visitors and pilgrims.*

—RB 66

CHAPTER 60 | *The Admission of Priests to the Monastery* Ordained Priests may enter the monastery, but under the same conditions and expectations of any person entering. Their priesthood does not afford them any special privileges.

CHAPTER 61 | *The Reception of Visiting Monks*

Visiting monks are welcomed as guests and are expected to accept the conditions and customs of the house. If the visitor has shown himself to be of a good and humble character, he may remain in that house as a new member of the community. A visitor from another known monastery can be accepted permanently only at the consent of the visiting monk's abbot.

CHAPTER 62 | *The Priests of the Monastery*

Members of the monastery can be ordained as priests. Such a brother must maintain all humility in his new position and retains his previous rank based on seniority.

CHAPTER 63 | *Community Rank*

Rank in the community is based on the date of entry of the brother. The abbot may adjust the ranking to his liking but should adhere whenever possible to the order of date of entry. Age alone does not determine rank. Younger monks (according to this ranking) are to respect their seniors and seniors to love their juniors.

CHAPTER 64 | *The Election of an Abbot*

The abbot is elected by the community. "Goodness of life and wisdom in teaching" are the criteria. The newly elected abbot must bear in mind the responsibilities of his office. He must admonish, reprove and encourage, being careful that in "rubbing too hard to remove the rust, he may break the vessel." The abbot must himself keep the rule in all its particulars.

CHAPTER 65 | *The Prior of the Monastery*

Only if necessary to complete all the many tasks in a monastery, the abbot may appoint a brother as prior. The prior's authority extends from the abbot and he is responsible to the abbot in all things. In no way should the appointment be a cause for pride or conceit.

CHAPTER 66 | *The Porter*

The porter of the monastery is a kind of gatekeeper and greets visitors and pilgrims. In this chapter, it is also mentioned that the monastery should contain all it needs (water, mill, garden) within its walls, if at all possible, so that the brothers do not need to leave the monastery unless by necessity.

CHAPTER 67 | *Brothers Sent on a Journey*

Brothers sent on a journey obtain the blessing of the community before leaving and prostrate themselves upon returning for the faults. Returning brothers may not share with any member of the community, other than the superiors, the details of the journey.

CHAPTER 68 | *Assignment of Impossible Tasks*

If a brother is assigned a task he cannot do, he should accept it humbly nonetheless. He may quietly present the reasons for his difficulty in performing the task to the superior but is expected to do his best if the superior determines he can.

IMPOSSIBLE TASKS

If a brother is assigned a task he cannot do, he should accept it humbly nonetheless.

—RB 68

CHAPTER 69 | *The Presumption of Defending Another Monk*
No monk may defend another in the monastery.

CHAPTER 70 | *The Presumption of Striking another Monk at Will*
No monk may strike or excommunicate another unless authorized by the abbot.

CHAPTER 71 | *Mutual Obedience*
Obedience is a virtue to be proffered to all, not just the abbot. Juniors, however, are expected to respect and obey seniors.

CHAPTER 72 | *The Good Zeal of Monks*
Benedict warns of a "wicked zeal" which separates from God and a "good zeal" that separates from evil. Each is to support his brother patiently and with understanding regardless of weaknesses. No one seeks solely what is best for himself but instead addresses the needs of others. "Let them prefer nothing whatever to Christ."

CHAPTER 73 | *This Rule only a Beginning of Perfection*
In this chapter, Benedict calls his rule, "this little rule that we have written for beginners." For further edification, he recommends the Old and New Testaments, Conferences and Institutes of the Fathers (Cassian), the writings of other Church Fathers as well as the Rule of Basil. For those "hastening toward your heavenly home," this Rule and these other writings show the way. ❖

BIBLIOGRAPHY **BOYD, THEOPHANE**

Sundays at the Magic Monastery. New York: Lantern Books, 2002.

Homilies of Theophane Boyd: Homilies from the Trappists of St. Benedict's Abbey. New York: Lantern Books, 2012.

KEATING, THOMAS

The Mystery of Christ: The Liturgy as Spiritual Experience. Amity, NY: Amity House, 1987.

Intimacy with God: An Introduction to Centering Prayer. New York: Crossroad, 1994.

Contemplative Prayer: Traditional Christian Meditations for Opening to Divine Union. Boulder, CO: Sounds True, 1995.

Invitation to Love: The Way of Christian Contemplation. New York: Continuum, 1995.

Centering Prayer in Daily Life and Ministry. London: Continuum, 1997.

The Human Condition: Contemplation and Transformation. New York: Paulist Press, 1999.

The Better Part: Stages of Contemplative Living. New York: Continuum, 2000.

Fruits and Gifts of the Spirit. New York: Lantern Books, 2000.

St. Thérèse of Lisieux: A Transformation in Christ. New York: Lantern Books, 2001.

The Daily Reader for Contemplative Living: Excerpts from the Works of Father Thomas Keating, O.C.S.O.: Sacred Scripture, and Other Spiritual Writings. New York: Continuum, 2003.

Manifesting God. New York: Lantern Books, 2005.

Open Mind, Open Heart: The Contemplative Dimension of the Gospel. New York: Continuum, 2006.

Divine Therapy & Addiction: Centering Prayer and the Twelve Steps. New York: Lantern Books, 2009.

The Thomas Keating Reader: Selected Writings from the Contemplative Outreach Newsletter. New York: Lantern Books, 2012.

Homilies of Thomas Keating. New York: Lantern Books, 2012.

MENINGER, WILLIAM A.

The Loving Search for God: Contemplative Prayer and the Cloud of Unknowing. New York: Continuum, 1994.

The Process of Forgiveness. New York: Continuum, 1996.

The Temple of the Lord and Other Stories. New York: Continuum, 1997.

Bringing the Imitation of Christ into the Twenty-First Century. New York: Continuum, 1998.

The Committed Life: An Adaptation of the Introduction to the Devout Life by St. Francis de Sales. New York: Continuum, 2000.

Sundays at the Magic Monastery: Homilies from the Trappists of St. Benedict's Monastery. New York: Lantern Books, 2002.

The Way of Forgiveness. Boulder, CO: Sounds True, 2002.

1012 Monastery Road: A Spiritual Journey. New York: Lantern Books, 2005.

St. Benedict's Monastery: Snowmass, Colorado. New York: Lantern Books, 2005.

A Joyful Noise: A Monastic Approach to the Psalms. New York: Paulist Press, 2010.

Julian of Norwich: A Mystic for Today. Great Barrington, MA: Lindisfarne Books, 2010.

All Manner of Things: Lectio Divina with Julian of Norwich. Pecos, NM: Dove Publications, 2012.

PHOTOGRAPHY CREDITS   JILL SABELLA: v, 1, 11, 12, 13, 14, 24, 28, 39, 40, 42, 43, 45, 46, 48, 50, 54, 63, 64, 73,74, 75, 80, 87, 88, 105, 108, 109, 111, 114, 115, 117, 118, 119, 125, 128, 137, 143

John Ruzicka: O.C.S.O.: ix, xi, 2, 4, 6, 8, 16, 18,19, 20, 22, 25, 31, 33, 44, 47, 52, 56, 59, 60, 62, 66, 69, 70, 76, 81, 82, 84, 88, 91, 106, 107 *(Fr. William)*, 116, 120, 132

St. Benedict's Monastery: 61, 65, 77, 94, 97, 98, 101, 102, 117 *(Br. Aaron)*

David Hiser: 17, 23, 26, 41, 78 | Curt Carpenter: 99, 100

Br. Aaron Cotter: 51, 92 | Mark Fuller: 12 *(meadowlark)*, 57

Fr. Joseph Boyle: vi | Ferenc Berko: viii | Trish Gates: 72 | Paul Green: 34

DESIGN   Curt Carpenter

COLOPHON   This book is set in Bembo, a modern font based on a design by the Italian punchcutter Francesco Griffo (1450–1518) and named for the Venetian poet and priest Pietro Bembo (1470–1547).

The display font is Cloister, a contemporary typeface based on Jenson, a font cut in 1475 by French printer and type designer Nicolas Jenson (1420-1480).

PRINTED BY VERSA PRESS | EAST PEORIA, ILLINOIS

CPSIA information can be obtained
at www.ICGtesting.com
Printed in the USA
LVHW071102020920
663973LV00032B/153